DIME NOVELS

EARLIEST TYPE OF DIME NOVEL
A BEADLE'S "YELLOW-BACK."

(See page 259)

ĐIME • NOVELS;

OR,

FOLLOWING AN OLD TRAIL

IN

POPULAR LITERATURE

BY EDMUND PEARSON

BOSTON
LITTLE, BROWN, AND COMPANY
1929

BALLADE OF DIME NOVELS[1]

By *Arthur Guiterman*

GONE are the tales that once we read!
  And none that come within our ken
May equal those that filled the head
  Of many a worthy citizen
  Who thrilled with boyish rapture, when,
In retribution stern, but just,
  "The deadly rifle spoke — and then
Another redskin bit the dust!"

We had no malice, not a shred;
  For which of us would hurt a wren?
Not blood, but ink was what we shed;
  And yet, we bore ourselves like men!
  With Buckskin Joe and Bigfoot Ben
In clutch of steel we put our trust,
  Until, deprived of oxygen,
Another redskin bit the dust.

[1] Reprinted by permission of Mr. Guiterman.

[v]

DIME NOVELS

On moccasin with silent tread
    We tracked our foes through marsh and fen.
We rescued maidens, sore bestead
    From savage thrall and outlaw's den.
    We feared no odds of one to ten,
Nor hatchet stroke nor bowie thrust,
    While still, in wood or rocky glen,
Another redskin bit the dust.

ENVOI

Take up the long neglected pen,
    Redeem its valiant steel from rust,
And write those magic words again:
    "Another redskin bit the dust!"

CONTENTS

ILLUSTRATIONS

ILLUSTRATIONS

PART I

INNOCENT YOUTH

I

THE PIONEER

"Touch but a hair of her head, and by the Lord that made me, I will bespatter that tree with your brains!"

This is from page ten of the first dime novel. It took twenty or thirty years for such exciting sentences to move up until they became the first words on page one. Then, according to a beloved tradition, the stories opened:

"Bang!

"Bang!

"Bang!

"Three shots rang out on the midnight air!"

And this progress represents the history of the dime novel.

The tale which contains the remarks about "a hair of her head" coupled with the threat to bespatter the tree with brains, opens in sober fashion. Here is its peaceful beginning:

"The traveller who has stopped at Catskill, on his

way up the Hudson, will remember that a creek of no insignificant breadth washes one side of the village."

The writers of the early dime novel were reverently following the lead of Cooper and Scott, and had not the slightest intention of composing "sensational" fiction.

This book — the first of thousands of similar little pamphlets — is called "Malaeska: the Indian Wife of the White Hunter." Not even the title is in the tradition, since the first word is a bit difficult to pronounce, and the set formula for the secondary title had not yet been adopted.[1]

"Malaeska" is a thin little book, of one hundred and twenty-eight pages. It is about six inches high and four inches broad. A man could carry half a dozen of them in as many pockets, without disturbing the appearance of his clothes. The covers were of saffron paper, — the book was "a yellow-backed Beadle." This phrase was used in reproach, and was resented by the head of the firm of Beadle, who indignantly explained that the covers of his books were not yellow at all, but orange in color.

It is a stirring tale. On the twelfth page a "savage

[1] It came only eight weeks later, with Number 5, "The Golden Belt; or, The Carib's Pledge." This double title, with semicolon and comma, was a fixed rule for thirty or forty years.

sent forth a fierce wild yell of agony, and springing up with the bound of a wild animal, fell headlong."

And in Chapter II there is a fine old-fashioned fight:

Sternly arose the white man's shout amid the blazing of guns and the whizzing of tomahawks, as they flashed through the air on their message of blood. Above all burst out the war-whoop of the savages, sometimes rising hoarse, and like the growling of a thousand bears; then, as the barking of as many wolves, and again sharpening to the shrill, unearthly cry of a tribe of wildcats. Oh, it was fearful, that scene of slaughter. Heart to heart, and muzzle to muzzle, the white man and the red man battled in horrid strife.

The trees above them drooped under a cloud of smoke, and their trunks were scarred with gashes, cut by the tomahawks which had missed their more deadly aim. The ground was burdened with the dead, and yet the strife raged fierce and fiercer, till the going down of the sun.

In the midst of the fight was William Danforth, the white hunter. And I am delighted to read that,

"Many a dusky form bit the dust and many a savage howl followed the discharge of his trusty gun."

Thus, in the Indian fight, and in some of the phraseology, especially in the early chapters, the book follows the popular ideas of a dime novel.

[5]

In no other way does it do this. It is not a cheap and gory tale, the work of a literary hack. Instead, it is by a writer so eminently worthy, so assured of her own dignified position in American letters, that I have been unable to think of a novelist of to-day with whom to compare her. Except in the fleeting character of almost all literary reputations, there are few points of resemblance between any contemporary author and this romancer of 1860.

Something like majesty surrounds the name of Ann Sophia Winterbotham Stephens, author of "Malaeska." There was nothing at all about her to coincide with our fancy of the typical writer of dime novels. She was both editor and novelist; her work with the *Portland Magazine* had led to successive posts in New York, where she had helped edit or establish *The Ladies' Companion, The Ladies' World,* and other magazines for women, and she had been associated with general periodicals like *Graham's* and *Petersen's*. When her works were published in a uniform edition, it was in twenty-three volumes. At the time of the appearance of "Malaeska," she was already the author of a number of romances, published at the conventional price of $1.50, and bound, decorously, in boards.

For years, school children recited her poem, "The

Polish Boy." When she made her tour of the Orient and of Europe in 1850, she received "marked attentions" from members of royal and noble families, as well as from Thackeray, Dickens, Humboldt, and others eminent in literature and science. She had "the first *salon* in New York" and was described as a woman of unusual attainments and fascinating personality.

Yet, by strange chance, this lady who must be described by the words so dear to her own time — this lady who was so "highly respectable " — was to lead off a series of books whose general name was to become a synonym for a literary pestilence. This safe counsellor for the young wrote the first of a long line of books which by many earnest but ill-informed persons were directly blamed for the moral downfall of hundreds of young men.

It is clear that few of us have anything but a misty idea what the words "dime novel" mean. Try them on a boy of ten or fifteen of to-day, and you will discover that to him the words mean nothing at all. He has never seen, probably never heard, of a dime novel. His older brother, of twenty or more, has perhaps heard the name, but that is all. The man from thirty to fifty years old says:

DIME NOVELS

"Dime novels? Oh, of course they were before my time. I used to read the 'nickels,' the 'nickel libraries' or the boys' weeklies."

You must go to the man of sixty, seventy, or even eighty, before you will find one who can say:

"Yes; I read the old Beadle Dime Novels as they came out."

The first dime novels were published nearly seventy years ago, and the original series came to an end at least fifty-five years ago.

They were sensational in much the same sense that Scott and Cooper are sensational; that is, they were tales of adventure and combat. There is nothing more grotesque than the charge that they were "immoral," since they were so amusingly strict in their moral standards. They were brief historical novels, or romances of love and warfare, written by authors who were well up in the second rank of writers of their time.

They were enormously popular and paid the usual price of this popularity: to be regarded with suspicion by many stern moralists and to be sneered at by the supercilious type of critic.

Before it appeared as a book, "Malaeska" had been a prize story in *The Ladies' Companion* — another fact which makes it hard to fit Mrs. Stephens' story into the picture as a dime novel.

As an example of its style, consider this passage. Danforth, the white hunter, is fatally wounded in the fight with the Indians, and is found lying in the woods by his wife, Malaeska. The scene is on the Hudson River, and the period, the eighteenth century, when Indians, in blankets and feathers, were still walking the streets of New York.

The poor Indian girl heard the voice, and with a cry, half of frenzied joy and half of fear, sprang to his side. She flung her child on the grass and lifted her dying husband to her heart, and kissed his damp forehead in a wild, eager agony of sorrow.

"Malaeska," said the young man, striving to wind his arms about her, "my poor girl, what will become of you? O God! who will take care of my boy?"

The Indian girl pushed back the damp hair from his forehead, and looked wildly down into his face. A shiver ran through her frame when she saw the cold, gray shadows of death gathering there; then her black eyes kindled, her beautiful lip curved to an expression more lofty than a smile, her small hand pointed to the West, and the wild religion of her race gushed up from her heart, a stream of living poetry.

"The hunting-ground of the Indian is yonder, among the purple clouds of the evening. The stars are very thick there, and the red light is heaped together like mountains in the heart of a forest. The sugar-maple gives its waters all the year round, and breath of the deer is sweet, for it feeds on the golden spirebush and the ripe berries. A lake of bright water is there. The Indian's canoe flies over it like a bird high up in the morning. The West has rolled back its clouds, and a great chief has passed through. He will hold back its clouds that his white son may go up to the face of the Great Spirit. Malaeska and her boy will follow. The blood of the red man is high in her heart, and the way is open. The lake is deep, and the arrow sharp; death will come when Malaeska calls him. Love will make her voice sweet in the land of the Great Spirit; the white man will hear it, and call her to his bosom again!"

A faint, sad smile flitted over the dying hunter's face, and her voice was choked with a pain which was not death. "My poor girl," he said, feebly drawing her kindling face to his lips, "there is no great hunting ground as you dream. The whites have another faith, and — O God! I have taken away her trust, and have none to give in return!"

The Indian's face drooped forward, the light of her wild, poetic faith departed with the hunter's last words, and a feeling of cold desolation settled on her heart. He was dying on her bosom, and she knew not where he was going, nor that their parting might not be eternal.

The dying man's lips moved as if in prayer. "Forgive me, O Father of mercies! forgive me that I have left this poor girl in her heathen ignorance," he murmured, faintly, and his lips continued to move though there was no perceptible sound. After a few moments of exhaustion, he fixed his eyes on the Indian girl's face with a look of solemn and touching earnestness.

"Malaeska," he said, "talk not of putting yourself and the boy to death. That would be a sin, and God would punish it. To meet me in another world, Malaeska, you must learn to love the white man's God, and wait patiently till He shall send you to me. Go not back to your tribe when I am dead. Down at the mouth of the great river are many whites; among them are my father and mother. Find your way to them, tell them how their son died, and beseech them to cherish you and the boy for his sake. Tell them how much he loved you, my poor girl. Tell them — I can not talk more. There is a girl at the settlement, one Martha Fellows; go to her. She knows of you, and has papers — a letter to my father. I did not expect this, but had prepared for it. Go to her — you will do this — promise, while I can understand."

Malaeska had not wept till now, but her voice was choked and tears fell like rain over the dying man's face as she made the promise.

He tried to thank her, but the effort died away in a faint smile and a tremulous motion of the white lips — "Kiss me, Malaeska."

The request was faint as a breath of air, but Malaeska heard it. She flung herself on his bosom with a passionate burst of grief, and her lips clung to his as if they would have drawn him back from the very grave. She felt the cold lips moving beneath the despairing pressure of hers, and lifted her head.

"The boy, Malaeska; let me look on my son."

It is apparent that we are dealing with Indians of an exalted type: the noble savages who were discovered in America by M. Chateaubriand.

Malaeska takes her son to the city, but her claims to him are not recognized by his white relatives. Her life henceforth is sad, and her pathway one of sacrifice. She returns to her tribe and by them is condemned to die. She is given into the care of one of the chieftains, with the understanding that he is to lead her into the wilderness and put her to death. He is, however, an old suitor, and really intends to be merciful and allow her to escape.

"Malaeska, the river is broad and deep. The keel of your boat leaves no track. Go! the Great Spirit will light you with his stars. Here is corn and dried venison. Go in peace!"

She kisses his hand and says:

"Farewell; Malaeska has no words; her heart is full."

Then the chief decides to propose:

"Malaeska, my wigwam is empty; will you go back? It is my right to save or kill."

Malaeska points to the sky.

"*He* is yonder, in the great hunting-ground, waiting for Malaeska to come. Could she go blushing from another chief's wigwam?"

He strikes a noble attitude, and they part in heroic abnegation.

The book surprisingly ends in tragedy; in the death of Malaeska and her son, just as he is about to be married to a white girl. So here is another reason why the critic who abhors the "happy ending" should stint his condemnation of the first of the dime novels.

II

THE TIMES

THERE was something oddly appropriate, it seems to me, in the fact that the first of these books was published in June, 1860. Dime novels were to be tales of dread suspense; of the calm before the storm; but rather more of the storm than of the calm. In their pages, during the next four decades, tons of gunpowder were to be burned;

human blood was to flow in rivers; and the list of dead men was to mount to the sky. They dealt in violent action; in sudden death and its terrors.

And Mr. Beadle published the first of them at the beginning of that summer which was to be the last peaceful season America was to know for five years. Already the first ominous event had occurred: Lincoln had been nominated at Chicago a week or two earlier. The Democrats had held a troubled series of conventions and named two sets of candidates for the presidency. And at Baltimore, the forgotten Constitutional Union Party had nominated the forgotten ticket of Bell and Everett. Had these two gentlemen been successful in the canvass, we might not know to-day the great names of Lincoln and Lee and Grant. But possibly we should not have had four years of civil war; while the curse of slavery might have been removed by the slow and peaceful action of time.

There was in the White House a portly old gentleman with a plume of white hair, and a head always a little tipped to one side, so that he reminded one of an elderly cockatoo. This was Mr. Buchanan of Pennsylvania, whom an observing critic calls "the most miserable presidential figure in American history."

All during Buchanan's administration the country was steadily drifting toward civil war. The President gave a sublime example of conciliation, of what may be accomplished by that quality sometimes called tact. He said that no State had any right to secede, but if it did so, no other State had any right to stop it. He was the typical "Northern man with Southern principles" by whose aid the South ruled the nation.

President Buchanan, says the same observer (Carl Schurz), had a cunning twinkle in his eye, as if he had a secret understanding with you. He wore a white neck-erchief like a clergyman. He had done the slave power abject service, and there were at least three members of his cabinet who were conspiring with the secession party. He remained neutral, helpless, while the country advanced toward war.

He had a pretty niece, Miss Harriet Lane, who was his hostess at the White House and helped him entertain the great delegation of Japanese ambassadors who amazed the country that summer — strange, impassive noblemen, in Oriental robes, who were regarded by the wise Americans with good-natured amusement.

Later in that same year there arrived a more interesting personage: the nineteen-year-old Prince of Wales. Mr.

Buchanan cocked his wise-looking head, and Miss Lane, in her hoop skirt, played at ninepins with the young Prince and the gentlemen of his suite.

The Prince was popular in America, and this was well, for there had been some ill feeling in England and this country over an event of the spring. This was the fight between Sayers and Heenan, at Farnborough in April.

Harper's Weekly, on May fifth, had a picture of what it called the "Bloody, Brutal and Blackguard Prize-Fight." But all its blood and brutality did not keep *Harper's* from printing a two-page picture, and there was great competition in the illustrated papers for sketches of the fight.

The gigantic steamer, the *Great Eastern,* came into New York harbor that summer. She was there when Hicks, the pirate, was hanged on Bedloe's Island in the presence of thousands of people. Hicks was not much of a pirate, but he had murdered three men, and his own demise was not widely regretted.

As the summer went on, the visit of the Prince of Wales and the presidential election were the chief topics of interest. The editor of the *Atlantic Monthly,* James Russell Lowell, wrote that the *Atlantic* had preferred ex-Governor Seward of New York for candidate of the new Republican Party, but that now there was no doubt that Mr. Lincoln of Illinois deserved support from those who hoped to free the slaves.

Mr. Lincoln himself stayed at home and refused to tour the country or to make a great many speeches. His supporters, however, aroused enthusiasm by torchlight parades in which tall men marched, carrying rails, in honor of the "rail-splitter" candidate. And the "Wideawakes," men wearing capes and carrying torches, trudged down Broadway during the cool October evenings.

III

BOOKS AND READERS OF THE DAY

THE rise and progress of the dime novel has not detained the formal historians and critics of literature, and probably there is no reason why it should do so. Popular literature, and its enjoyment, is seldom the concern of the scholarly critic, until three or four centuries have passed. It is a social phenomenon rather than a matter of artistic achievement. But it is interesting to consider what America was reading in the spring and summer when there began to issue from William Street, in New York, the first of these little pamphlets which were to swell into such an enormous flood of printed pages.

Nathaniel Hawthorne had come home to America, after years in England and Italy. His new novel, "The Marble Faun," was reviewed in the *Atlantic* for May. Hawthorne was depressed, like most of his friends, over the growing breach between the States, but rather inclined to let the South go, if it wished to go. At all events, he would be loyal to his old friend, ex-President Franklin Pierce, although the latter was denounced as one of the last of the "dough-faces," — the Northern men with Southern principles.

A serial was running in the *Atlantic,* called "The Professor's Story." It was later published as "Elsie Venner." I suppose it would be rash to call it a great novel, but I will record my opinion that it is one of the most interesting works of fiction by an American writer — chiefly because it contains that element of *ghostliness* which Lafcadio Hearn declared to be an essential element in literature.

The *Atlantic* published in September a poem by Longfellow: "The Children's Hour." In April, however, a stranger and more novel poem had been published in those pages. It was called "Bardic Symbols," and its appearance there was one of the many early recognitions in New England of Walt Whitman. When we are making out the indictment against Bostonian prudery, we must take care to omit all mention of this, as well as of Emerson's and Edward Everett Hale's welcome to the great poet — or else our case will lack strength.

Whitman himself was in Boston all that spring, reading the proofs of the Thayer and Eldridge edition of his poems. It was perhaps earlier in the same year that he and Emerson walked up and down the path on Boston Common for two hours, one bright winter's day, discussing "Children of Adam."

Harper's Magazine, in that year 1860, was publishing Thackeray's "Lovel the Widower," and a review of "The Mill on the Floss," whose author, it was discovered, was "a lady named Evans," although she preferred to call herself George Eliot. In *Harper's Weekly* were running "The Woman in White" by Wilkie Collins and "The Uncommercial Traveller" by Charles Dickens.

Readers who liked softer, tenderer stuff could find, in *Godey's Lady's Book,* Mary W. Janvrin's "The Frozen Heart;" a series called "Aunt Tabitha's Fireside," by Edith Woodley; and "Jessie Turner's Fortunes," by an

[19]

author of considerable importance in our present investigation: Metta Victoria Victor.

For lighter amusement, New York had its illustrated weekly, *Vanity Fair* — a paper with no especial similarity to the present magazine of that name, except that it also had some admirable writers. Artemus Ward, for instance, was contributing the brief articles, whose humor has not yet vanished. A year or two later some of these skits were to cheer the burdened heart of Lincoln and shock his cabinet ministers, as he delayed reading to them the Emancipation Proclamation in order to give them the chance first to enjoy Ward's "High-handed Outrage at Utica," with its account of the attack on the image of Judas.

The American citizens who read these books and magazines, who discussed the exciting prospects of the 1860 campaign, were rather different from Americans of to-day. Ill health seems to have been the rule among them. English travelers, from 1850 to 1860, were struck by what they thought the unhealthy pallor of the Americans. To many foreign visitors, we seemed a sad people.

Aside from a certain amount of hunting and fishing, there was far less outdoor exercise than at present. Ath-

THE ATTACK ON THE EMIGRANT TRAIN

Drawn by F. O. C. Darley for Beadle's Star Journal

letics was not a prominent feature, even of college life. The cooking, generally, was bad. And to many fashionable folk, country life meant the veranda of a hotel at Saratoga or Newport.

City life, however, if less varied and amusing, was certainly quiet and peaceful, judged by our standards. To any one looking at these old files of newspapers and magazines, and trying to imagine the scene, there is something mellow and pleasant about those late spring days, when every one was unaware that the nation was headed directly toward the greatest disaster in its history.

IV

AFLOAT AND ASHORE

ONCE the Beadles began to publish "dollar books for a dime," they came along nearly every fortnight. The second was "The Privateer's Cruise, and the Bride of Pomfret Hall" by Harry Cavendish. As the hero's name is the same as that of the author, it is safe to conclude that this is the first of the pseudonyms which were to be used so much in the history of dime novels.

It was an age when a fictitious name was part of the

equipment of half the authors. A room in the psycho-
pathic ward awaits any one who tries to unravel all their
mystifications, and when those ingenious sleuths, the
library cataloguers, give it up, less patient persons need
not be expected to tear off the masks of all the novelists. Some of them emulated "Ferret, the Man of a Million Disguises."

"The Privateer's Cruise" is a story of ocean adventure
as such stories were written in the days before the rise of
Clark Russell — and far indeed from the method of
Conrad. In it, the hero is just leaving Boston harbor on
the Yankee privateer *The Arrow*. It is at the outbreak of
the Revolution.

Cavendish has, as one of his messmates, the jolly Irishman, O'Hara. There are also the quartermaster, usually
referred to as "The old water-rat"; and the bos'n who
perpetually says "Ay! ay!" and "energetically squirted
a stream of tobacco juice from his mouth as if from a
force-pump." He also says "I'm no scollard" and now
and then ends his speeches with the assurance that
"Them's my sentiments."

O'Hara gives the "greenhorns" some painful advice
about seasickness, and tells them all to obey their su-
periors. He adds, with fine loyalty:

"The captain's a gentleman. God bless him!"

But — "the first lieutenant, I've a notion, is a sour sinner."

They are hardly out of Boston before they run into a storm and sight a brig in distress. She is in a bad way, and Mr. Cavendish exclaims:

"God of my fathers! Every soul will be lost!"

"Heave her to!" thundered the officer of the deck. "For life or death, my lads! Up with the foresail — down with your helm — brace up the after yards — set the mizzen staysail there."

In the course of this chapter they rescue the brig's crew and passengers, and thus get on board their own ship "two females, with their protector, an elderly gentle-manly looking man."

"Both the females were young and beautiful, but one was surpassingly lovely."

They wish to know who sighted their ship and was thus their "preserver."

"The captain, taking me by the hand, said,

" 'Mr. Cavendish has that enviable honor,' at the same time presenting me.

" 'Cavendish!' exclaimed a silvery female voice in de-lighted surprise."

[23]

It turns out to be his old playmate Annette!

" 'Cavendish — what, little Henry Cavendish. Yes! it is even so, although the years that have passed since you used to visit Pomfret Hall have almost eradicated your features from my memory. God bless you, my gallant young friend! We owe you our lives — our all.' "

The reader should observe that even on the storm-swept deck of a privateer in time of war, the well-bred personages in this dime novel were not only capable of polite conversation, but of such sophisticated language as "eradicated your features from my memory." Nor was this confined to the landsmen. At a later period in the story, the captain, in a moment of great stress, remarks:

"I can see nothing there but a dense, impenetrable shadow!"

The hero is deeply moved by the utterances of the elderly gentleman, and says:

"The scene that ensued I will not attempt to describe. Suffice it to say that I retired that night with a whirl of strange emotions at my heart."

So here they are, with the first difficulty of the sea-novelist cleared up, and the heroine safely on board by the end of Chapter I. Her brother, Stanhope St. Clair, had been the schoolmate of Cavendish. St. Clair was "the heir of a wealthy and ancient family, whose residence, not far from Boston, combined baronial splendor with classic taste."

Here, Cavendish had known Annette, "a sweet-tempered, innocent fairy, four or five years my junior." He says that he "experienced emotions toward her which I am even now wholly unable to analyze but they came nearer the sentiment of love than any other feeling."

The females and their protector are set ashore at Newport. As this occurs at only Chapters II and III, it is needless to say that the love affair has not progressed. Something has always stood in the way. Both girls must have been reading the old romances, for Annette makes remarks to the other female like, "Fear not, sweet coz," and to one of the officers: "God bless you and our other defenders."

The other girl makes a more extended speech when they disembark:

"There, now, do your *devoir* like a gallant knight and soldier — coz, have you no glove or other favor for him to wear on his bosom in battle? Ah, me! The days of courtesy and chivalry have gone forever."

When the civilians have gone, the cruise proceeds. The privateersmen cut out some merchant ships, under the convoy of a British fleet. The captain "springs into the mizzen-rigging" and replies to a hail, "in the light of a battle-lantern."

["Battle-lanterns!" They certainly do bring back recollections of the days when I was far more concerned about the War of 1812 and its naval fights than I am now. Was there a special rack in which they were kept, between battles, and was anybody caught lighting one of them for noncombatant purposes severely punished? Did they burn with a dull, red glow, suggesting the infernal fires? There is much virtue in the words "battle-lanterns!"]

Well, the captain replies to the hail from another ship:

"This is the 'Aurora' commissioned by the good commonwealth of — "
"Give it to the canting rebel," roared the British officer; "fire — for God and St. George — FIRE!"
"Ay! fire, my brave boys," thundered our leader; "one and all, for the old Thirteen — FIRE!"
The bos'n after the first broadside, shouts:
"Give it to the varmints. Huzza for old Nantucket!"

They sail south, and fight a pirate, and rescue a lovely young creature of seventeen, with long golden tresses and blue eyes. The hero is wounded and nursed back to health by the beautiful Ellen Neville. He almost forgets Annette. Six months later he comes back to the West Indian port and finds Ellen dying. Her illness is not specified, but we old cynics know that it will be a fatal disease: she is Heroine Number Two in a proper romance.

"I am but a poor bruised reed," she says.

Tears fell from them both "like rain." She dies, blessing him.

Cavendish then has a cruise on a small schooner and takes part in many fights. The scuppers run with a dark red stream of blood. He returns to Boston and attempts to visit Pomfret Hall. As he approaches, he learns that one of Mr. St. Clair's daughters is to be married that very day. With the lack of energy and good sense which invariably marks the hero in such circumstances, he concludes that it is Annette and turns sadly away.

"Fool that I was to think that the wealthy heiress could stoop to love a penniless officer."

He goes back to his ship, and has more adventures, and takes part in more battles. The ship is struck by lightning, and there is a harrowing experience in an open boat, with much description of weather. Finally, he returns once more, finds Annette still unmarried, and wins her hand, as he had already won her heart.

All of these adventures, and this happy culmination are skilfully packed into one hundred and twenty-eight small pages.

"Alice Wilde: the Raftsman's Daughter. A Forest Romance" was the fourth of the series and its inclusion showed that there was an intelligent search for variety. The author was Metta Victoria Victor, an experienced novelist of her day, who was also the wife of the editor of the house of Beadle. To Orville J. Victor, the editor, there was due a great deal of credit for the success which the firm enjoyed; some of those who were familiar with its history felt that his knowledge of what the readers wanted was the chief cause of the publishers' amazing prosperity.

"Alice Wilde" begins with one of those bits of rustic speech which were so dear to writers of this school:

"That ar' log bobs 'round like the old sea-sarpint," muttered Ben Perkins to himself. . . . "Blast the thing! I can't tackle it nohow."

The period of this novel is practically that of the date of publication; the scene somewhere in Michigan, on a river not exactly identified. The wealthy "Gothamites"

are contrasted unfavorably with the more virtuous rural
folk. There is more or less talk by a Negro — the usual
romantic Negro of that time — who always said
"Massa."

Another early dime novel (it came out in 1861) was,
like "Alice Wilde," a variant from the typical story of
frontier life or of the sea. This was "Madge Wylde, the
Young Man's Ward; or, Lights and Shadows of Orphan
Life," by the author of "Clifton," "Pride and Passion,"
etc. The author was May Agnes Early Fleming, and the
tale is of a crossing sweeper in New York, who rises to
fame as an author, and also achieves a happy marriage.

The publisher's "blurb" for this book is itself instruc-
tive:

This delightful romance is a thorough daguerreotype
of certain phases of high and low life, which are very
rarely correctly told. It is the story of an orphan, rescued
from the pestilential vicinage of the "Old Brewery," in
New York; transported to a gay and brilliant home
where *fashion,* as it is, reigns triumphant; spending all
her years to young womanhood in the midst of associa-
tions which call to light all the shadows of the varied
scenes; and, amid all, a story of love and devotion, which
is characterized by great beauty, pathos, and excitement.

In Number 7, "The Reefer of '76; or, The Cruise of the Fire-fly," Harry Cavendish comes again with a story closely resembling his "Privateer's Cruise." He sails out of New York, instead of Boston, but once more he is on a Yankee privateer, with a merry Irish messmate. He rescues a beauty in distress from the clutches of a pirate, and, in the last chapter, marries her. There are fights with English ships; the usual haughty Englishmen; and the usual crying of "Huzza!" Two novelties are introduced: one, a good description of the naval attack upon the forts of Charleston; and the other, cruises with Paul Jones, including the battle of that commander with the *Serapis.*

A reader who has the conventional idea of dime novels — and especially one who has never seen the early publications of Beadle — will, I think, read the following passage with surprise. It is from "The Reefer of '76," and shows Mr. Cavendish in tender mood.

It was not till the third day after parting with the brigantine, that Miss Derwent, with her maid, appeared once more upon the deck. The shock of her uncle's death had brought on an illness, which confined her during that time to the cabin; and even now, there was a languor in her fine countenance, and a melancholy in her dark eye, which, though they added to the interest of her appearance, betokened the acuteness of her grief. She was attired in a dark silken dress; her hair was plainly braided back, and she wore no ornaments of any kind whatever. Rarely had I beheld a vision of such surpassing loveliness. I stepped forward to assist her to a seat. She smiled faintly, her eyes sparkled a moment, and then a deep blush shot across her saddened features. But I will not detail the scene that ensued. Suffice it to say that, from that moment I loved Beatrice; and that though she had not bid me hope, there was nothing in her conduct to bid me despair. . . .

How often has the story of the heart been told! The history of the love of one bosom is that of the millions who have alternated between hope and fear since first the human heart began to throb. The gradual awakening of our affection; the first consciousness we have of our own feelings; the tumultuous emotions of doubt and certainty we experience, and the wild rapture of the moment, when, for the first time, we learn that our love is requited, have all been told by pens more graphic than mine, and in language as nervous as that of Fielding, or as moving as that of Richardson.

The daily companionship into which I was now thrown with Beatrice was, of all things, the most dangerous to my peace. From the first moment when I beheld her she had occupied a place in my thoughts; and the footing of acquaintanceship, not to say intimacy, on which we now lived, was little calculated to banish her from my mind. Oh! how I loved to linger by her side during the moonlight evenings of that balmy latitude, talking of a thousand things which, at other times, would have been void of interest, or gazing silently upon the peaceful scene around, with a hush upon our hearts it seemed almost sacrilege to break. And at such times how the merest trifle would afford us food for conversation, or how eloquent would be the quiet of that holy silence! Yes! the ripple of a wave, or the glimmer of the spray, or the twinkling of a star, or the voice of the night-wind sighing low, or the deep, mysterious language of the unquiet ocean, had, at such moments, a beauty in them, stirring every cord in our hearts, and filling us, as it were, with sympathy not only for each other, but for everything in nature. And when we would part for the night, I would pace for hours my solitary watch, thinking of Beatrice, with all the rapt devotion of a first, pure love.

In the late summer of 1860 the country around New York was covered with signs bearing the inscription:

"Who is Seth Jones?"

These were posted on barns, fences and stone walls.

A little later, in the same places, there appeared a picture of a hunter in fringed buckskin tunic and leggins, with a coonskin cap and musket. The sign now announced:

"I'm Seth Jones."

This meant that the advertising department of the firm of Beadle — if such a department there was — had decided to plunge heavily. The house had bought a manuscript (for seventy-five dollars) which it was to publish on October first.

On that date the book appeared: "Seth Jones; or, the Captives of the Frontier" — another little orange pamphlet, of one hundred and twenty-three pages, with the full-length drawing of the hero on the cover and repeated as frontispiece. Once again the literary judgment and business instinct of the Beadles had been sound. The book sold sixty thousand copies immediately, and four or five hundred thousand before the end. It was translated into a number of foreign languages: some enthusiasts say into eleven.

The author, who brought his manuscript in person, was a young man of nineteen, a native of Ohio, but at that time a school-teacher in Trenton. His name was Edward S. Ellis — and one does not have to be an aged person to recall the time when that name was signed to books of frequent appearance.

Mr. Ellis, pleased by the success of his first novel, and by that of the dozens that he wrote for the same house, started a literary career which lasted until his death in 1916. He wrote more than a dozen series of juvenile stories, comprising about one hundred and fifty volumes. He was the author of histories of the Civil War, of Indian wars, of a general history of the United States, and of biographies of many notables, including Admiral Dewey and Thomas Jefferson. His "Deerfoot" series was one of his most popular achievements.

His home was for many years in Montclair, New Jersey, but he died in Maine. In his industry and enormous production he was the typical writer of dime novels, but he often rose far above the average in quality, and his graduation into historical writing of a respectable order also sets him apart from his fellow writers of yellow-backs.

To be included in "Who's Who in America" is a modest distinction for an author, but Mr. Ellis was one of those dime-novelists whose name used to be found therein. The biographical dictionaries were not, as a rule, hospitable to writers whose works were all small pamphlets, in paper covers. But before many years had passed the author of "Seth Jones" had accomplished the feat which the brotherhood used to describe as "getting between boards."

AFLOAT AND ASHORE

"Seth Jones" opens with a lonely settler, Alfred Haverland, felling trees in the forest in western New York. The time is soon after the Revolution, and the region is infested by Indians. To him comes a mysterious stranger in a coonskin cap. He introduces himself thus:

"How de do? How de do? Ain't frightened, I hope; it's nobody but me, Seth Jones, from New Hampshire."

Seth has been a scout, during the war, under Colonel Ethan Allen. His voice is strangely squeaky; his favorite expression is, "Fact, by gracious!" He now warns Haverland that he and his family are in great danger from the Indians. The settler is impressed by the advice, and prepares to desert his log cabin and remove from the neighborhood. There are Mrs. Haverland, Alfred's sister Mary, and his daughter Ina. The girl is only fifteen or sixteen years old.

They all embark in a boat, but have not yet put off, when Ina jumps ashore again. She wants to take a little run to stretch her legs, but of course she does not use any such indelicate word as "legs." She says "to ease my limbs." There follows an odd incident which illustrates how the narrative has to be compressed in these brief novels:

"Ina! Ina! what do you mean?" asked her father sternly.

"Oh, nothing; only I want to take a little run to ease my limbs."

"Come back here instantly!"

"Yes — oh, father! quick! quick! come take me!"

"Seize the oar and shove out!" commanded Seth, springing into the water and shoving the boat off.

"But, for God's sake, my child!"

"You can't help her — the Injins have got her. I see 'em; drop quick, they're goin' to fire! look out!"

The proximity of danger and the rapid sequence of events is rather puzzling to all who are not used to the dime-novel style. On the next page this story also exhibits one of the cardinal principles of ethnology as it was understood by this school of writers.

"Oh, father! mother! The Indians have got me!" came in agonized accents from the shore.

"Merciful God! must I see my child perish without heeding her cry?" groaned Haverland in spirit.

"No, they won't hurt her, and we must take care of ourselves while we can."

Thus said Seth Jones, and it showed that he perfectly understood the dime-novel Indian. Their maiden captives might be in deadly peril of their lives; they might even have to undergo the torture of the blazing pine splinters; they might be scalped or burned at the stake — but their honor was as safe as if they were in a convent. The Indians were, all of them, gentlemen. A thousand paleface damsels were captured by red-skinned warriors, during the progress of the dime novel, and some of them may have suffered death or grievous torment. But not one of them, Heaven be praised, ever came through the experience otherwise than as *virgo intacta.*

The Indians who had captured Ina were Mohawks. Seth and the other white men call them "imps" and, in moments of great irritation, "varmints." So severe a term as "devils," however, was never permitted to the characters in these books, at this early period. "Devils" savored of profanity, which was strictly forbidden.

Seth Jones leaves the Haverlands and sets out alone to do what he can to rescue Ina from captivity. He meets a white man named Graham, and together they follow the savages. They find their camp and are peering at them, down an embankment, when Seth, with apparent clumsiness, rolls down the incline and lands helpless in the midst of his enemies.

There is an intervening chapter — to keep the reader in suspense — and to describe the escape of Graham.

Then we are told how the Indians amused themselves with a few preliminary tortures of Seth Jones — plucking out his hair by the roots. He bears this with a stoic heroism which pleases the Indians.

The savages around did not suppress a murmur of admiration. Seeing no effect from this torture, the tormentor again stooped and caught another tuft that grew low upon the neck. Each single hair felt like the point of a needle thrust into the skin, and as it came forth, the Indians seated around, noticed a livid paleness, like the track of a cloud, quickly flash over their captive's countenance. He looked up in his tormentor's eyes with an indescribable look. For a moment, he fixed a gaze upon him, that savage as he was, caused a strange shiver of dread to run through him.

To say that Seth cared nothing for these inflicted agonies would be absurd. Had the savage dreamed what a whirlwind of hate and revenge he had awakened by them, he would have never attempted what he did. It was only by an almost unaccountable power that Seth controlled the horrible pains of both body and mind, he suffered. He felt as though it was impossible to prevent himself from writhing on the ground in torment, and springing at his persecutor and tearing him limb from limb. But he had been schooled to Indian indignities, and bore them unflinchingly.

His temple had the appearance of white parchment with innumerable bloody points in it, as the blood commenced oozing from the wounds, and his neck seemed as though the skin had been scraped off! His momentary paleness had been caused by the sickening pain and the intensest passion. His look at the savage was to *remember him*. After the events which have just transpired, they remained seated a moment in silence. At last, one who appeared to be the leader, addressed, in an undertone, the Indian whom we have just seen retire from the post of tormentor. Seth, however, caught the words, and had he not, it is not probable he would have successfully undergone the last trying ordeal.

The same savage again stepped forward in the circle before the helpless captive, and removing the cap which had been replaced, clinched the long, yellow locks in his left hand, and threw the head backward. Then whipping out his scalping knife, he flashed it a second in the air, and circled its cold edge around his head with the rapidity of lightning. The skin was not pierced, and it was only an artifice. Seth never took his eyes from the Indian during this awful minute.

The tormentor again retired. The savages were satisfied, but Seth was not. He handed his pipe back, replaced his cap, and rising to his feet, surveyed for a few seconds the group around. He then addressed the leader.

"Can the white man now try the red man's courage?"

The voice sounded like another person's. Yet the chief noticed it not, and nodded an assent to the request, while the looks of the others showed the eagerness and interest they felt in these dreadful proceedings.

The savage who had inflicted all this agony, had seated himself directly beside the chief. Seth stepped to him, and grasping his arm, pressed it moderately. The Indian gave a scornful grunt. Seth then stooped and gently took the tomahawk from his belt. He raised it slowly on high, bent down till his form was like the crouching panther ready to spring. The glittering blade was seen to flash as it circled through the air, and the next instant it crashed clean through the head of the unsuspecting savage.

There follow other intervening chapters, while we are left to wonder how the Indians bore this tomahawking of their comrade. Graham meets the Haverlands and also a man named Haldridge, who has lost wife and children in an Indian raid, and is out for revenge.

They catch a glimpse of Ina, in a canoe with her captors, and start in pursuit. Seth Jones, in the meantime, has been spared temporarily by the chief, both for his courage and because he is supposed to be mad. They all set off through the woods, and their party is soon joined by the three warriors who have Ina in their charge.

The other white men get on their trail, and there is some interesting description of scouting, of remarkable woodcraft, and of reading signs by broken twigs, and the like. It was because of incidents of this kind that Mark Twain called the Leatherstocking Tales the "Broken Twig" series.

Seth leaves messages behind him, scratched on flat stones. They are written in a great hurry and always in peril of discovery, but humorously signed "Yours respectfully, Seth Jones," or "Yours, in haste, but nevertheless with great respect, Seth Jones, Esq."

The white men surround the Indian camp. Graham kills the sentry, and wearing his clothes, sits down at the camp fire beside Seth. Then he cuts the thongs that bind Seth's feet. By surprise they seize Ina and make their escape.

Haldridge has an encounter in a log with a rattlesnake, which *charms* him and nearly causes his death. During the retreat of the white people, they have need for a raft to get Ina across the river. In the hunt for a log, Seth again shows his woodcraft.

Haldridge went up the river, and Seth and Graham went down. Graham soon noticed a large, half-decayed log, lying partly in the water. "Just the thing, exactly! Why it's a raft itself. This will save further trouble. Let us launch it at once, and float it up to the spot," he said delightedly.

The two approached it, stooped, and were in the very

act of lifting it into the water, when Seth suddenly removed his shoulder, and arose to the upright position.

"Come, give a lift," said Graham.

"Graham, I guess I wouldn't take the log, I don't think it will answer."

"Won't answer? Why not? In the name of common sense, give some reason."

"Let the log alone! Do you understand?"

Graham looked up, and started at the appearance of Seth. His eyes fairly scintillated and he seemed ready to spring upon him, for daring to utter a word of dispute.

"Come along with me!" commanded Seth, in a voice hoarse with passion.

It wouldn't do to disregard that command; and, taking up his rifle, Graham lost no time in obeying it. But he wondered greatly whether Seth was suddenly crazy or foolish. He followed him a short distance, and then hastened up beside him. Seeing that his face had recovered its usual expression, he gained courage and asked what he meant by such commands.

"Didn't you take notice that that log was holler?"

"I believe it was, although I did not examine it closely."

"Wal, if you *had* examined it closely or even loosely, so that you took a peep into the log, you'd have seen a big Mohawk curled up there snug and nice!"

"Is it possible! How came you to see him?"

"The minute I seed the log was holler, I had my s'picions that there might be something or other in it, and I made up my mind that we shouldn't undertake to lift it till I know'd how it was. When I come to look closer, I knowed thar was something sure enough, for the way the bark was scratched at the mouth showed that plain enough. It wouldn't do, you see, to stoop down and peep in, for like as not the redskin would blaze away smack into my face. So I jest dropped my cap, and, as I stooped down to pick it up, I kind of slewed one eye 'round over my shoulder, and, as sure as blazes, I seen a big moccasin! I did, by gracious! I then proceeded to argufy the question; and, after considerable discussion, both in the affirmative and negative, I came unanimously to the conclusion that as I'd seen an Injin's foot, if I'd foller it up, I'd be pretty sure to find the Injin himself; and, moreover, also, if there was *one* Injin about, you could make up your mind that there are plenty more not far off. By gracious! If I hadn't looked a little ramparageous, you wouldn't have let go that log so very quick, eh?"

There is still more marching, scouting, and maneuvering, in storms, by day and night, along rivers and in the deep forest. Finally they reach a white man's settlement and are safe. They devoutly give thanks to God. Graham and Ina have fallen in love and are to be married.

Seth Jones makes himself known to Mary Haverland

[43]

as her old lover. She promptly faints. Her brother glances at Seth and exclaims:

"Merciful Heaven! Eugene Morton!"

Seth, or rather Eugene, speaks no longer in his squeaky tone, but in a "rich, mellow bass." He explains the reason for his masquerade. He had loved Mary ten years before, in New Hampshire. After the battle of Bunker Hill, in which he was reported to have been killed, he learned that Mary had married a "deserter." So he disguised himself and set out to discover the facts. The novel ends in two or three weddings and an old-fashioned dance.

In short, "Seth Jones" was, for the audience to whom it was addressed, a good story, and an astonishing feat for a boy of nineteen. It has most of the elements of popularity. It is easy for the jaded reader to smile at Seth's simple and rather unnecessary masquerade; at the old-fashioned humor (such as Seth's repetition of "Fact! by gracious!") and at the conflicts with the Indians. But the novel amused thousands of boys and men, as well as other people, for many years, and may be doing so to-day. A new edition — in board covers — was published as recently as 1907.

V

SUCCESS

THERE is no need to look for abstruse reasons for the immediate success of the Beadle dime novels, any more than we need to wonder why America's most popular five-cent magazine is bought in such enormous numbers to-day.

The dime novels offered stories of adventure and love at the lowest price then known. They were not for persons of consequence to read in their libraries, but for boys, for travelers, for soldiers, for sailors, for brakemen on the railroads, and hunters in camp.

They were light and easily carried in the pocket. It has often been pointed out — and this will be mentioned again — that they could be read in school, concealed from the teacher by an arithmetic; or in church, hidden in the hymn books; or in the presence of one's parents, camouflaged behind some permitted magazine.

Anybody with the slightest knowledge of the wide appeal of popular fiction will not need to be told that the reading of dime novels was not exclusively confined to boys, or to rude and uncultivated men. Stories of this type have always been enjoyed by everybody, except a very small class of persons. Men who have been named as readers of the Beadle novels include Lincoln, Seward, Henry Wilson, afterwards vice-president, and Robert Toombs, the Confederate statesman. Henry Ward Beecher is said to have commended some of them, while Senator Chandler gave Ellis's "Oonomoo, the Huron" an emphatic endorsement. The man who didn't like it, he said, was not fit to live.

Of course, the literary opinions of statesmen are notoriously fallible, but so are the literary opinions of every one else — including literary men.

The standing order of the American News Company, which handled the Beadles, was for sixty thousand copies as each new one appeared. A second edition might be called for in a week; some of the novels went through ten or twelve editions. The price was low, but the amount paid to the authors was not excessive — we have seen that Mr. Ellis got seventy-five dollars for "Seth Jones." At that time, however, he was without any literary reputation. Later, the firm would pay him two hundred and fifty dollars for a novel of forty thousand words. They paid Mrs. Stephens two hundred and fifty dollars for the right to reprint "Malaeska" in book form.

SUCCESS

In 1884, Mr. Victor, the editor, said that he paid better "in proportion to the quantity of matter we accept" than the *Atlantic Monthly*. This was said in conversation with a correspondent of the *Boston Evening Transcript,* who felt crushed to the earth in shame. Said Mr. Victor:

"We won't touch a story that isn't worth $50, and it ought to bring $75 or $100. That's a $75 story you have there — 'Antelope Abe; the Boy Guide'. . . For the dime size, containing 75,000 words, we never pay less than $150, and from that to $250; the average is $200."

Mayne Reid was the prize exhibit for the high prices paid for his work, and the Beadle firm published a facsimile of the receipt signed by Reid, acknowledging the payment of seven hundred dollars for the copyright and sole rights of publication of "The White Squaw." They called this "a large price for a story of its length — a greater sum, we may say, than was ever before or has since been paid for a novel of similar word quantity." [This was said in 1889.]

The transaction took place in 1868; "The White Squaw" was about fifty thousand words long, and was published that year in the series of "20 Cent Novels," stories longer than those sold for a dime.

It should be remarked that the authors gave up all

rights in return for these sums; but it should also be re-marked that the sales took place in the eighteen sixties and eighteen seventies.

Mr. Victor felt that his firm had preserved Mayne Reid.

"He would have sunk into obscurity if we hadn't sustained him. He has written certainly fifty stories and sketches for us. He was working for us exclusively for eight or nine years. We made a double number of his 'Scalp Hunters,' one of his most popular stories, reprinting it at his request. He retained, of course, the English rights in his works. We never paid him less than $600 for a story; that was the standard price, though we may have paid him more at times. I remember he brought his 'White Squaw' down here one morning and said he must have $700 for it, and we gave him a check without reading the manuscript. . . . Reid was always in monetary troubles, but he was a prolific writer, and when he got hard up he would dash off sketch after sketch, and come down here with his pockets stuffed. Here is a lot of his manuscripts now that have never been printed on this side."

The Civil War was a fortunate event for the Beadles. Their books went to the soldiers by the million. I think

The Scalp Hunters

BY CAPT. MAYNE REID.

BEADLE AND ADAMS, PUBLISHERS, 98 WILLIAM ST., N. Y.

(See page 264)

that a generous number of these were given by the publishers, but there were also enormous sales. The little books were sent to the camps in bales, like firewood. They were shipped on freight cars, wagons and canal boats. When bundles of them arrived in camp, the sutler had to distribute them quickly, or else they would be torn from him. Among the commodities which the Union and Confederate pickets exchanged between the lines the Beadle novels were in great demand. Pathetic stories are told of blood-stained copies of dime novels found on dead men on the battlefield and of great numbers of soldiers who were buried with the novels in their pockets.

VI

BEADLE THE FOUNDER

THE idea of publishing novels of twenty-five thousand to thirty-five thousand words in length, and selling them at ten cents apiece may have originated with Mr. Beadle or with his editor, Mr. Orville J. Victor. The credit is usually given to the head of the firm, but nobody denies Mr. Victor's contribution to the success of the house by which he was employed for about fifty years.

DIME NOVELS

Erastus Flavel Beadle was born in Otsego County, New York (Cooper's country) in 1821. He was the son and grandson of Connecticut men; his grandfather having been a Revolutionary soldier. His early ancestors in this country lived and died in Massachusetts — in Salem.

While working on a farm in Chautauqua County, he learned to cut letters from blocks of hard wood, in order to label bags of grain. This interested him in printing, and he finally studied that art with Elihu Phinney of Cooperstown. With this master printer he learned type-setting, stereotyping, and the printing and binding of books. He started a stereotype foundry and then a printing office in Buffalo in the 1840's, and in 1852 issued in that city *The Youth's Casket*. Later, he founded a monthly magazine, called *The Home Monthly*.

His brother, Irwin P. Beadle, had been in the news business in Buffalo and had made a success of selling ballads and songs, on single pages — in the old style, as they used to be peddled by the ballad-hawkers. Erastus Beadle published a number of these songs in a pamphlet, called "The Dime Song Book." Its success made the brothers think. In 1858 they moved to New York to try the idea of selling dime books.

ERASTUS F. BEADLE   ROBERT ADAMS   IRWIN P. BEADLE

THE FIRM OF BEADLE AND ADAMS, 1862

The firm was formed of Beadle and Adams, consisting of Erastus and Irwin Beadle, and a business associate of theirs in Buffalo, Robert Adams. The books issued by them bore successively the names of I. P. Beadle and Company, Beadle and Company, and Beadle and Adams.

They occupied various quarters on William Street, New York, at last Number 98, a structure of brick, four stories high. It is described, in its later years, as "a worm-eaten old building," whose site, and the site of several other ancient offices, has long been occupied by a modern building.

The firm published "Joke Books," "Year Books and Almanacs," "Letter Writers," "Housewives' Manuals," "Debaters and Books of Fun." In the third of these is "Jim Smiley's Frog," the first edition, in book form, of Mark Twain's "Jumping Frog." There were handbooks of games — manuals of riding, cricket, football, skating, and croquet. There were songbooks, and "dime-speakers." There were also biographies: the "Lives of Great Americans," including an early life of Abraham Lincoln, by Mr. Victor. This was in press when Lincoln was assassinated, and the author hastily added a prefatory memorial notice which is remarkable for its just estimate of the man. All, or nearly all of these were small, paper-covered books, priced at ten cents each. Many of them are rare to-day, since, like the dime novels, they were read to pieces and thrown away.

The firm published newspapers and periodicals: *Belles and Beaux,* a weekly; *Girls of To-day; Young New Yorker;* and *The Saturday Star Journal.* The last, with several changes of name, was published for twenty-seven years.

In 1862, Irwin Beadle's share in the firm was bought by the other partners. He is described as "a kind-hearted man, but addicted to drink." For a time, he was a dangerous business rival. Robert Adams died in 1866, and his younger brothers, William and David, succeeded him. David Adams was remembered as handsome and genial; William, his brother, as "grumpy" — due, perhaps, to the fact that he had lost an ear. For twenty years Erastus Beadle and the two younger Adamses carried on the firm with great success, in the face of severe competition.

The various series which they published, following the original "yellow-backs," are numerous and confusing, with the "Pocket Novels," the "Boy's Library of Sport, Story and Adventure"; the "New Dime Novels";

the "American Tales"; and "Frank Starr's American Novels."

The last do not, on their face, seem to have any con-nection with the house of Beadle, as they are larger in size and different in appearance from the others. It was all a trick of trade: Frank Starr was Beadle's foreman, and his address, as given on the cover, Number 41 Platt Street, was the side door of Beadle's manufactory.

There were also the *Pocket Library,* the *Half-Dime Library* (with over one thousand titles), and the *Dime Library,* (with nearly as many). These changes were made, in the course of thirty years, to meet trade condi-tions and to comply with postal regulations. Only the collector, to-day, cares about the differences between all these types and varieties.[1]

The middle-aged man, who possibly has never seen one of the old "yellow-backs," is most apt to remember the names of Beadle and Adams as they appeared in the eighteen seventies, the eighteen eighties and eighteen nineties at the head of a dingy little magazine with a stirring picture in black and white on the front cover.

[1] They are catalogued and described in "The Beadle Collection of Dime Novels, given to the New York Public Library by Dr. Frank P. O'Brien." New York, 1922. (Published by the New York Public Library.) Also in the catalogue of Sale Number 1500, May 10, 1920, "American Pioneer Life," Anderson Galleries, 489 Park Ave., New York.

These magazines, the *Dime Library* and the *Half-Dime,* were about the size of *Life* or *Punch.* The *Pocket Library* was similar in appearance, but less in size.

The picture on the front cover, showing a man with a bowie knife, repelling single-handed the charge of a bull bison, or Mustang Sam, standing on the back of his galloping mustang and light-heartedly firing his rifle — this drawing was often the work of George G. White, a versatile artist, who could turn from making pictures for the *Police Gazette* and with equal skill embellish the pages of the *Christian Herald.*

There was a middle period, between the yellow-backs and the unattractive magazine form, when the firm was still permitted by the post office to publish its novels as little paper-covered books. Some of the most pleasing were printed in these years — beginning about 1869. These were the "Pocket Novels," with covers in color, and often partly colored by hand. Around the picture was a gay border in red, green or blue.

The "New Dime Novels," the "20 Cent Novels," and "Frank Starr's American Novels," all of the middle period, were also issued with colored covers — gaudy and joyous to the young.

David Adams died in 1886, and Erastus Beadle retired

three years later, turning the business over to William Adams as sole owner.

Mr. Beadle took with him a large fortune which he still possessed at the time of his death. He had built a house, romantically named "Glimmerview," on the shores of the lake in Cooperstown, and here he enjoyed five more years. He had sufficient vigor in 1892, and at the age of seventy or thereabouts, to make a canvass for a seat in Congress, but he was not elected. He died in 1894.

That his name was more or less forgotten — although still appearing at the head of some of the Libraries — is indicated by an editorial article in the *Brooklyn Eagle* (December 27, 1894).

A few days ago occurred the death of Erastus Flavius [sic] Beadle. . . . To the younger generation this fact was without significance, but to those whose memories go back to war times the name of Beadle will associate itself with small, yellow covered books . . .

The business faltered until 1897–1898, when it failed, and was purchased by M. J. Ivers and Company, who continued the use of the name of Beadle and Adams for some years thereafter.[1]

[1] Mr. Beadle's name is omitted from the usually hospitable pages of the new "Dictionary of American Biography."

PROPRIETY RAMPANT

IT was "Maum Guinea," by Mrs. Victor, which is said to have been praised both by Abraham Lincoln and Henry Ward Beecher. Its full title was "Maum Guinea, and her Plantation Children; or, Holiday-week on a Louisiana Estate. A Slave Romance." It is a good-humored story of slave life, double the size of the usual dime novel, and was published, about 1861, at double the price. Mrs. Victor had a long career as a writer and was greeted as a prodigy of genius when, at the age of eighteen, she wrote "The Senator's Son." About sixty thousand copies of that book were sold in the late eighteen forties.

The American Revolution was a favorite theme with N. C. Iron, one of the writers in the earliest series.

Iron's "The Maid of Esopus; or, The Trials and Triumphs of the Revolution" centers upon the country near the Hudson River and the expedition of Burgoyne. Marcus Goodheart is a lieutenant in an English regiment, stationed in New York. He perceives near his quarters, one evening, a boy playing a guitar. As the youth is inside the sentry lines, Marcus suggests that he is in danger of arrest. This conversation ensues:

[56]

"Will you befriend me, sir? You first heard and saw me. If my object had been insidious, I should have remained in silence. But I love the Muses, and I am desirous of dwelling for a time among those who appreciate them so highly."

"But surely you are not homeless?" said Marcus.

"Oh, no," said the boy; "I have a home."

"Where?" asked Marcus.

"Not far from here — upon the Highlands of the Hudson," said the boy.

"What caused you to quit your home?" said Marcus.

"A roving spirit — an erratic impulse," replied the boy. "Why should I remain? I am adjudged too young, too weak, too delicate to fight. The men of our village are gone forth to battle for the sweets of liberty, and could I remain to be reproached by the significant glances of the fair maidens whom they have left behind them?"

"Am I to infer that your village is opposed to the king's forces?" said Marcus.

"Oh, yes," replied the boy, "they favor their own sovereignty."

"Then you are a young rebel," suggested Marcus.

"Nay, that is a harsh term, sir," replied the boy; "but I will not forswear my country, though there be danger in the avowal. We want to govern ourselves, and to dispense with your authority in England. All boys, when they come to manhood, seek to direct their own affairs, and are generally competent to the task. So a colony, when it finds the parent State querulous and avaricious,

[57]

and grasping at all the profits of the co-partnership, is apt to be discontented and inclined to dissolve the union."

"Where got you that rhetoric, boy?" demanded Marcus.

"It is the teaching of our village, sir," replied the boy; "and upon this principle our chief male population have marched to the battlefield."

As a matter of fact, the "boy" is Isabelle, daughter of Silas Fearnought of Esopus, New York. And when a British expedition is engaged in destroying Esopus, there occurs a stirring encounter between Lieutenant Goodheart and Adam Morton, a dauntless young American. Isabelle is alarmed.

She almost leaped from the portico, hastened across the grassy lawn, and despite their pointed swords, she fearlessly cast herself between the infatuated men. They stood confounded, while she exclaimed:

"May I ask, gentlemen, the cause of this ferocity? The right by which you convert my garden into your battlefield? Would Adam Morton presume to violate the hospitality of the house of Silas Fearnought upon a gentleman who was partaking of its security, be he of a hostile or a friendly race? And, Lieutenant Goodheart, is a lady's parlor a becoming place to whisper defiance to an antagonist?"

PROPRIETY RAMPANT

Astonishment at the fearless conduct of Isabelle awed them into submission, and her sweet voice made each combatant feel that he was in error.

"Isabelle," said he whom she had termed Adam Morton, "I have been impelled by the injuries which we are suffering from this implacable foe, to presume upon the privileges of your house."

"And for the discourtesy of which I have been guilty in your presence, Miss Fearnought," said Marcus, "I supplicate your pardon; but — "

"No reservation, Lieutenant Goodheart — all is forgotten," said Isabelle. "But our village is on fire, our people homeless, and your men are the incendiaries. Hasten for your life or you are lost. The fury of the injured inhabitants will be visited on you. And, Adam Morton, give me your assurance that you will not impede Lieutenant Goodheart's flight."

"I promise, Isabelle," responded Adam Morton, instantly.

"One word, Isabelle," supplicated Marcus.

"Not a syllable," exclaimed Isabelle. "Let me implore you to begone. There is death in the delay of another minute. Adam, hasten and appease those friends who are approaching."

The novel traces the campaign of Burgoyne to its disastrous conclusion at Saratoga. Isabelle, however, is abducted by another admirer, a young Indian chief. While she is in the Indian village — treated, of course, with the most fastidious delicacy — she argues the case with an Indian girl.

"Why do you not love young chief?" the girl asked, one day. "He handsome — he great chief — very great — wise in every thing. He bring home much scalps — much fine things. He make wigwam very happy."

"Urge me no more, my sister," said Isabelle — "the association is repugnant to my feelings. To me his person has no beauty, nor his valor excellence. Those scalps, which you greet with such enthusiasm, are to me the trophies of barbarism, and the fine things which you think would confer happiness on his wigwam, would seem to me but the plunder of the slain. Why does not this young chief wed with a daughter of his tribe and color, who can appreciate his qualities? Why does he steal from her home a maid whose habits, feelings and predilections are so irreconcilable to his own? Why, my sister, does not he see those perfections in you as a woman that you so admire in him as a man, and grace his wigwam with you instead of me?"

Adam Morton, coming to rescue Isabelle, is made prisoner in the Indian camp, and Isabelle is given the usual choice: marry the young chief, or see Adam burned at the stake. Adam makes an eloquent speech at the council fire.

"I stand alone," said Adam, "without a friend, and at your mercy, for you are strong, just now, and I am weak. I know your judgment, for I behold it in yon pile of wood, though you afford me the semblance of a trial. You charge me with murder, when you know from the brave who eluded me that two balls missed my heart before I raised my rifle in self-defence. You charge me, too, with violating the sacred rites of hospitality, when I only, by a wile far less perfidious and more harmless than those you daily practice, attempted to redeem from bondage a daughter of my race, whom you violently forced from her home, to unite, against her wishes, to one of your braves. Your accusation is a mere subterfuge to slay your fellow-man, and your conduct that of demons. Think not that the remembrance of this deed will die with me. My ashes will cry out for revenge. In the dead of night, when your eyes should be sealed in slumber, all shall be wakefulness, alarm and horror, from the moment my restless spirit leaves this body. I will goad young and old alike — the chief, the brave, the squaw and the papoose — until there be none left, and your memory shall perish. Now do your villainy. Burn me at the stake, for the sooner I meet death the sooner I shall commence my work of vengeance."

Exciting scenes follow. Adam is led to his death, and Isabelle offers to sacrifice herself and marry her Indian suitor. She does not, so far as I can discover, even demand a properly witnessed ceremony by a Protestant clergyman. At the last moment, however, they are rescued by an English officer and a small detachment of men.

Some account of the campaign in New Jersey follows. There are many perils, encounters and marches, in which Goodheart, the Englishman, and Morton, the American, are alternately captor and captive, rescuer and rescued, with absolutely nothing to choose between them in courage and nobility of conduct, while Isabelle's conversation is always superb.

The heroine receives a formal proposal from Captain Goodheart — he has been promoted, but apparently Isabelle has not observed the alteration in his insignia. Or, it may be, that in the excitement of the campaign, he has been unable to procure the additional star.

"Oh, Lieutenant Goodheart," exclaimed Isabelle, "press me no more upon this painful subject. I esteem you. I am grateful for your kind protection when I was friendless and in peril, and your assistance to my brother when he was a helpless prisoner, and you knew not that he had interest in my heart. But my love, which you value far too highly, is reserved for my country — " Isabelle paused for an instant, and added, in a lower tone — "and its sons."

"Isabelle," exclaimed Marcus, "drive me not to distraction! Allow me not to infer that you have already pledged your heart."

Isabelle spoke not. The thoughts of Marcus were maddening, and he said, in a tone of voice more frightful than his previous accents:

"Isabelle, tell me, is your love another's, that I may not importune you vexatiously?"

"I spoke but in general terms," said Isabelle, her lustrous eyes cast down upon the floor, "when I referred to the sons of my country. My heart is individually free."

"That admission gives a vigor to my life," said Marcus with vivacity, "and an impulsiveness to hope."

In the end, Isabelle married Adam Morton (now a Major) and Goodheart returns to England and weds a fair English girl, named Flora. Twenty years later, his son, also named Marcus, returns to America and visits Adam, who is by this time a colonel. He falls in love with Morton's daughter, Isabelle. The marriage is celebrated, and, as Mr. Iron puts it: "The bride and bridegroom left America for England, where Isabelle soon became as prominent for her virtues as for her beauty."

The cruel charge of "immorality" which was brought against the dime novels cannot better be refuted than by quoting a few paragraphs from the "The Luckless Trapper; or, the Haunted Hunter," by William R. Eyster.

[63]

This is the situation: Edith Van Payne has been captured by the Indian chief, War Hawk. Please read what follows, and ask yourself if folk who only a few years ago read "The Sheik" with such delight, feel themselves pure enough to cast stones at Mr. Eyster's treatment of a similar theme.

Daylight waned, and the shadows deepened. In the west the crimson flames that flared over the mountains died away, and the night-stars began to shimmer in their field of blue. A moist, sweet wind came wandering up from the woods. Edith sat within her little prison-house alone.

From time to time she heard voices without; but they came to her as if in a dream. The cold look of the woman had deepened till her face seemed like crystalized water itself.

But in the frigidity of her eyes was a something that was suggestive of unfrozen depths beyond. There was no trace of despair — no sign of intense misery directly arising from her present condition like that which would have fallen upon some women. Only the traces of a former congealment were deepened; that was all. And so, she sat there in silence, thinking. So absorbed in her reverie was she that, apparently, she did not hear a footstep approaching the matting that did duty as a door to her cabin, did not notice the tall and graceful form of War Hawk, as he entered; and only awoke with a start to consciousness at hearing a voice, remarkably sweet and mild for one belonging to a son of the forest and plain, addressing her.

"The White Bird is sad, and the War Hawk would comfort her — yet he is afraid to come before her. She need not fear him. He is a great warrior, but would not harm her for many lodges and much of all that is dear to the heart of a warrior. Can the White Bird look upon the War Hawk with a smile? She will see him as gentle as a fawn, for she is dear to him, and what she says shall be music in his ear."

Edith suffered her eyes to rest steadily upon her Indian admirer, whose assumed gentleness could not disguise his stern, unyielding nature. So the woman thought, though her eye met his unflinching and undaunted.

"The White Bird may be sad, but it is the sadness of years. She asks neither favor nor kindness from the War Hawk. As she had protected herself in the past, so she can in the present and the future. She has been hurt to the heart so long ago that she has no soul for the great chief. Let him go his way and she will go hers."

The ghost of a smile flitted over the face of the brave at this request. This conquest of his had not been altogether bloodless, as the waters of Black Load stream could bear witness.

"The White Bird will grace the wigwam of the War Hawk, and those who have hurt her heart shall be forgotten. If they come near her again, let her speak the

word and they shall die. This arm will protect her; and
no woman will be more honored among my nation."

Edith looked curiously at the speaker. She measured
him with her eye and gauged his soul as he spoke. Perhaps she could see in this dashing red-skin something
to admire, even though there was nothing for one of
her race to love.

"The White Bird returns her thanks," she said, with
a graceful but sweeping courtesy. "The chief's wooing
is rough and his grip is like steel, but she knows the warriors of his tribe and their ways, and the War Hawk
may well be the greatest among them. He is pleasant
to look upon, and the squaw of his lodge will have the
eyes of many maidens turned upon her in envy; yet the
White Bird, as he has chosen to call her, has no heart
for him. Her soul rests with one of her own kindred.
Though she has not seen him for years, and will never
meet him again, yet her heart will ever beat time to him
— even though he knows it not, and little dreams that she
still lives. Let the War Hawk seek another; I am not
for him."

"The warriors of our tribe are not used to wooing as
are the pale-faces, and if War Hawk had sought the fair
one he loves as our warriors seek their squaws, she might
have thought his grip was stronger yet. He has handled
her tenderly and would ever do so; yet she should know
that she *must* be his. She is in his hands now, he will
have her taken into his tribe; he will guard her and care
for her; no other shall be so cherished. He has been in

danger from her people and his own for her and life has been lost to win her. Do you think, then, when he loves her so strongly, that he will open his hand when she is in it and let her fly away? No. The White Bird must forget her pale-faced friends — and — " his voice grew harder and colder, and there was a ring of savage fierceness in it as he spoke — "let her dream of her pale-faced lover no longer. If she should see him again it would be to destroy him, for he may not look on her face again and go away living. The War Hawk will let no eyes rest upon his pale-faced squaw in love."

Edith Van Payne realized more than ever the depth to which she had stirred the heart of her dusky-visaged admirer.

"War Hawk, you have wasted time in your pursuit, and you seek what will never, never be yours. There are fair maidens of your own race; woo them and win them — me you never can, by either kind words or by threats. I am protected by the Great Spirit, and neither hope nor fear. Your pursuit may bring you much of evil — to me it can only bring a new experience in life. Do not be deceived. I am, and of reason, a mystery to you, the solution of which it is dangerous for you to attempt."

War Hawk is baffled. But a worse defeat awaits him. Edith not only escapes, but also steals his horse. She gets out of the wigwam and springs upon the back of Whirlwind, his favorite steed.

[67]

The noble animal sweeps her back toward the mountains and safety. At the camp fire of the white people she finds Bill Blaze, "The Luckless Trapper," who exclaims:

"Minks and mushrats! Blam'd if she ain't Dick Martin's gal! A trump, by mitey! She's cleaned out the hull b'iling; stampeded ther corral, an's bringin' the pick o' the lot into camp! Bill Blaze an' her'll move inter Black Load camp rejoicin'. Waugh!"

When stories came to be written with boys as the chief characters there were two or three kinds of boys. There was a fairly likable and possible youth; there was the rather annoying Christian hero; and there were, especially in the later Weeklies, the prodigies of wisdom and valor.

In "Beadle's Boy's Library of Sport," Thomas C. Harbaugh contributed an early number called "Snow-Shoe Tom; or, New York Boys in the Wilderness." Mr. Harbaugh was to become one of the most prolific of all this school of writers, and he will be mentioned again.

His beginning is matter-of-fact enough:

"Let the reader spread before him a map of New England and permit his eyes to wander over the middle

portion of the State of Maine, or that part which lies between 45° and 46° of latitude."

If I had been reading this in the eighties, when it came
out, I should have skipped hastily over the opening, but
I believe that the rest of the story would have seemed
eminently readable. To have the cocksure boys from
New York learn a few things by painful experience and
by good-humored precept from the boy who lived in
the forest, would have seemed, to me, good doctrine.

And the adventures with wild animals were certainly
entertaining; if I could lose thirty-five years, I think
they might be called exciting. To kill a wolverine, for
example! Wolverines were not common where I lived,
but if I read about them, they remained in my mind. The
next time I walked home, over the Boston and Maine
Railroad tracks, after nightfall, and passed the First
Woods, it was comforting to have my Chicago air-rifle
under my arm. If there was a slight rustling in the
bushes — of course, it was probably a chipmunk, or one
of Ben Perkins' Plymouth Rock hens, a little late in
getting home. Yet — there *were* wolverines, as near as
Maine. You never knew.

In Mr. Harbaugh's story, three boys from Pough-
keepsie, New York, came to the hut of Snow-Shoe Tom,

in the Maine wilderness. He teaches them the use of snowshoes, and for a while they flounder and wallow in the drifts. They get a shot at a moose — but miss, as they have "buck fever." They meet Caribou Nick and listen to his tales of hunting. They themselves hunt and kill the esteemed wolverine. Afterwards there is a brush with fur thieves who are robbing traps. Likewise, a fight with eagles in their nest on Mount Katahdin. They catch that noble fish, the muskellunge, and finally they actually kill a bear.

The story is written in good, if occasionally slightly stilted English, and along with the narrative it contrives to impart much useful information on wood-craft.

Of another sort is "Honest Harry; or, The Country Boy Adrift in the City," by Charles Morris. Harry is from West Dover, also in New York State, and he arrives in New York City with a bundle on a stick, carried over his shoulder. He is both honest and manly looking, but this does not save him from frequent attacks by bands of hoodlums.

After much rude abuse on their part, with polite and calm rejoinders from Harry, and after he has shown himself — if they had had the wits to see it — infinitely their superior in manners and in repartee, they venture upon a physical attack. This is their grievous blunder, for he fights and beats them in bunches. Exactly how many it would take to overpower him we never learn — in one encounter, if I am not mistaken, he knocks out at least eight. This happens often in the course of his life in New York. For it should always be remembered that it was a settled principle of the dime novelist that the native New Yorker, or almost anybody in the city except the *recent* arrival from rural districts, was, with a few exceptions, an evil dastard.

Harry wanders not in the ways of the sons of Belial. He keeps his mother's Bible near him in his room and walks in godliness. He is not exactly an offensive prig, but his virtue and manliness are a little wearing.

At last, he proves to be heir to a fortune of $200,000 and "on coming of age enters the firm of Elwood, Holland & Co . . . and is now one of the most prosperous and highly respected merchants of the city."

It is plain that the author of "The Maid of Esopus," as far back as 1861, had attained a degree of intelligence which is still beyond the grasp of a recent mayor of Chicago. In writing about the War of Independence, he could make his Hero Number Two an Englishman, and did not think it necessary to suggest that courage and virtue are qualities possessed only by Americans.

From an early date, English authors helped compose American dime novels — and this before the novels spread to England and became known as the penny dreadful or the shilling shocker. If this nation had anything to do with foisting them upon Great Britain, she has had her revenge. That form of yellow journalism known as the tabloid newspaper was unknown in the United States until an American publisher took a tip from London.

There were a number of eminent dime novelists who were native British subjects. Mayne Reid, perhaps best of them all, was born in Ireland. Bracebridge Hemyng, to be mentioned later in this book as creator of "Jack Harkaway," was a barrister of the Middle Temple. And Frederick Whittaker, who was born in London in 1838, was one of Beadle's chief authors and defenders. He was here as early as 1850, and served as captain in the Civil War. He became greatly interested in all that pertained to frontier life; wrote a life of General Custer and engaged in a long controversy about that commander. This resulted in a military court of inquiry, in which Captain Whittaker was justified.

His story, "The Death's Head Rangers; a Tale of the Lone Star State," is concerned with the fighting between Texas and Mexico, and a volunteer company of Kentuckians who go down to help Texas. With them goes a comic Englishman of the Lord Dundreary type — the eternal "silly ass" who turns out to be a gallant fellow, and is always popular with readers or playgoers.

This one has side whiskers, a lisp, and all the accessories. On the Mississippi steamboat he fights and knocks out with one blow, Bill Yancey, the company bully. In an engagement with the Mexicans, the Englishman, who has steadily grown in favor, is at last called on to lead the Rangers in a charge and capture the Mexican guns. This he does with the dash and ability of an old campaigner; and he presently unmasks and appears as Colonel Medhurst of the Royal Artillery.

The clever man, the brave leader who for one reason or another appears in guise of a simpleton, is a favorite character in the dime novels. So also is the girl who, in order to be near her lover, puts on boy's clothes and follows him into war or other danger. In this story there are two such girls. Colonel Medhurst discovers their secret, and nothing could exceed the bashfulness and chivalry with which he helps them conceal the fact

[73]

that they are in the wrong costume. The rough Kentuckians almost match him in courtesy toward the young ladies.

It is another surprise to find that in these novels, written sixty or seventy years ago, the publishers sometimes allowed their authors to exhibit a spirit which was the reverse of a narrow patriotism. The Englishman points out that brave men understand each other anywhere; that no one nation has a monopoly of gentlemen or of good fighters, and his doctrine is endorsed by the examples of men of both countries.

One of the best passages in the book is a description of a shooting match which takes place in Kentucky, before the Rangers leave. They have been drilling on the green. When the company is dismissed, the commanding officer returns to his duties as innkeeper.

Colonel Biggs sheathed his trenchant blade, and started for the bar-room, unbuckling his sword-belt as he went. For him the labors of the day were just beginning, comparatively speaking.

Five minutes later, the same Biggs, who had been so nervously anxious on the subject of drill, was standing, jovial and hearty, behind his shining bar, mixing drinks with the hand of a master, while his sweating assistants, at their wits' ends in the confusion, were endeavoring to satisfy the thirsty and clamorous crowd of warriors.

"Hyar's to you, Cunnel," cried Bill Yancey, the "Bully of Kentucky" as he called himself. "Hyar's every ha'r off the old cat's tail, and may we all be hyar, next trainin'-day."

"Hyar's luck," says Harrod, more briefly, as he elevated the bottom of his glass to the ceiling, setting it down with a clash on the bar.

For several minutes the succession of applicants at the bar was steady and unceasing; and then, as the first crowd gave way to their unsatisfied comrades, the buzz of conversation grew loud in the room.

The subject was easily ascertained; for the many references to targets, rifles, and the names of noted shots, proclaimed that the forthcoming event of the day was to be a shooting-match.

"I'll bet on old Thunderer," cried Bill Yancey, patting his heavy rifle affectionately. "I kin shoot the ha'r off any man in this crowd."

"Whar's the documents?" suddenly demanded a shrill, squeaky voice from the crowd, in the momentary hush that followed Yancey's boast. "I'll bet yer, stranger."

Bill Yancey was an enormous fellow, standing several inches above the traditional six feet, in his moccasins. As the voice came from behind him, he turned to look over the crowd, and saw no one, at first, to whom such a voice could be supposed to belong.

[75]

"Who's talking?" he demanded, in a tone of contempt. "Let me see the man that wants to shoot ag'in Bill Yancey, the bully of Kentuck."

"Hyar I be, stranger," answered the same squeaky voice. "I'll bet any man in this craowd ten dollars, I kin put six balls aout of seven in the same ho-el, and hyar's the documents."

There was a parting movement in the crowd, as the woodman turned to see the author of this challenge, and Yancey beheld a little dried-up man, in a very dirty hunting-shirt that had once been green, wearing a mangy fur cap above a pair of twinkling black eyes, set in a nest of wrinkles amid a yellow, parchment-like face. This man was hardly five feet in height, and thin and wiry in build. His face was perfectly hairless, and his head was closely cropped. Altogether, he was a mean-looking little man, insignificant to a degree, whose only redeeming point was a look of sly humor on his wizen face. Standing close to the gigantic forester, hugging a rifle longer than himself, he extended a bunch of dirty dollar bills and repeated:

"I'll bet any man in this craowd ten dollars, I kin put six balls aout of seven in the same ho-el, every time."

"Oh, git aout!" said Yancey, contemptuously. "D'yer want me to tote yer daown to the river and draown yer, yer ornary little chipmunk? Why, you mout be shoved into a common bullet ho-el yerself, ef they sot yer in, eend-ways."

The little man's only reply was a variation of his old refrain, delivered in the same squeaky voice:

"Bet yer ten dollars, stranger, I kin put six bullets aout of seven in the same ho-el, and *hyar's the documents.*"

The third repetition of the challenge elicited a round of applause from the Kentuckians, who saw fun ahead, and Harrod shouted:

"Take him up, Bill. You've be'n blowin' 'round hyar 'bout your shootin', long 'nuff. Down with the dust, or back aout."

Yancey grew red in the face.

"Back daown Bill Yancey, the bully of Kentuck! Not fur all the shinplasters in Lexington Bank. Hyar, chipmunk, hyar's my pile, and I'll raise yer ten dollars. Bet yer twenty yer can't do it. No man kin put six bullets in the same ho-el, fa'r and squar'."

The little man dove into a pouch by his side, and produced three five-dollar bills, dirtier than the first bunch, and ragged too.

"I see yer, and raise yer five," he said, quietly.

Yancey hesitated a moment. Twenty-five dollars was a large sum out West, in those days. At last he said:

"I'll see yer, ef it takes my bottom dollar. I hain't got but twenty-three, but I'll put up my rifle fur the rest, darn me ef I don't."

" 'Tain't necessary, stranger," said the little man, quietly. "I'll trust yer ef ye *air* a blower. Who'll hold the stakes?"

"Give 'em to cunnel," suggested Harrod, as they stood by the bar. "Thar won't be any whisky drunk raound hyar, 'till this hyar bet's settled, and cunnel's a good judge of shootin'."

"Hold on," said Yancey, suddenly, and turning red. "Mebbe this hyar's a skin game, gentlemen. How far are yer to shute?"

He addressed the little man, who drew himself up proudly.

"I won't deny, stranger," he said dryly, "I *mout* skin yer ef I wanted, by droppin' the bullets daown a well, fur I didn't specify no kind of a ho-el. Moutn't I, gentlemen?"

There was an awkward silence, and Yancey began to look very silly. His antagonist evidently had him in a trap, if he chose, for it was obvious that any man could put six balls into the same hole without shooting one of them. A smothered titter began among the Kentuckians, which was suppressed when the "Bully of Kentuck" glared fiercely round, for Bill Yancey was dreaded by all. But the little man quietly continued his remarks.

"I ain't on the skin game, myself, stranger. Jake Rhett kin make ten dollars, fa'r any day, without any skin games. I'll shoot six balls into any tree you've a mind to name and make only one ho-el. Is that fair?"

"Fair enough!" "Good!" "Let's see it."

The crowd was growing impatient.

"And as fur distance, why, a hundred paces, in course, *reg'lar.*"

The satisfaction was general. Even Bill Yancey gave in, saying:

"Wal, stranger, ef ye kin du that, ye kin take my pile, and I'll knock under. I kin shoot, but I kain't beat that."

"Take the stakes, cunnel," said the little man, laconically as he handed the bills over the bar to the hotelkeeper, "I'm ready."

Bill Yancey handed over his own money, and then followed his little antagonist out of the room, in the midst of the crowd.

Outside, the green was full of people, and the news of the bet, and the wonderful shooting in prospect, spread like wildfire. The richer planters and citizens, with their wives and daughters, were taking lunch in the various vehicles grouped at the edge of the green, but as the news spread, there was a general desertion of eating, while horsemen and Amazons alike congregated on the end of the green where the match was to take place. . . .

Bill Yancey, after all his boasts, was not the man to back out from a contest he had invited. He stood out, rifle in hand, till the distance had been paced to a large tree, whose scarred trunk seemed to have been the victim of many former matches.

Around a spot on this tree, where the nail was usually driven, was a large circle, like a piece of sponge, so full was it of bullet-holes.

A moment later, a round board was hung up against this tree, in the center of which a spike was driven, half-way to the head.

The spectators gathered in two groups, one about the marksmen, the other a few paces to the left of the target. In those parts the shooting was too close to render this a risky proceeding.

[79]

Jake Rhett, as the little man had announced himself, stood leaning on his rifle in silence, watching Yancey.

The big hunter threw back his right foot, slowly raised his rifle to a level, and fired. The clap of the bullet on the head of the nail was distinctly heard at the firing point, and a shout came from the target.

"Driven home! Good shot!"

"Thar, chipmunk, kin ye beat that?" said Yancey, proudly.

The little man shifted the foot he was resting on.

"Kin ye put six balls out of seven in the same ho-el?" he asked, in the same squeaky voice as ever.

Yancey turned angrily away, saying:

"No, nor you, nuther."

"Why, ye ain't *thr'u?*" asked Jake Rhett, in his quavering whine, "I thought you was goin' to shute at least three balls, fur the honor of old Kentuck."

"Whar do *you* come from?" growled Yancey, in answer.

" 'Way down in ole Tennessee," said the little man, placidly. "Hev ye finished, stranger?"

"Yes. I druv the nail fa'r and squar'," said the hunter, doggedly. "You beat it, ef ye kin."

The little man turned on his heel and marched to a bench close by. On the bench lay a bundle, done up in an old ragged red-cotton handkerchief. So dirty was its external appearance that no one had touched it, and its smell was decidedly strong. This bundle the eccentric hunter opened, and disclosed three onions, two small hoecakes, a little paper parcel, and a number of loose bullets, with some round patches of deer-skin. With as much care as if the contents of the bundle had been diamonds, Jake Rhett extracted the little paper package therefrom, opened it, and discovered it full of very fine gunpowder. Amid a hush of amused curiosity, the old fellow put a bullet on the palm of his left hand, and poured just sufficient powder to hide it from view.

Then he poured the powder from this primitive measure into the muzzle of his long rifle, and put the bullet in his mouth. Drawing the rammer and selecting a patch, he wrapped up the wet bullet, and rammed it home, patch and all, with a few vigorous shoves.

Extracting a cap from a case in the stock of the rifle, he turned round.

"Naow, stranger," he said, "I'm going to put these six bullets into one ho-el, on top of yours, jest as I said, or you kin take my pile."

Then the little man took five more bullets out of the bundle, and tied up the handkerchief again, leaving only the powder inside.

"Why don't you take another bullet?" asked Colonel Biggs, who had been watching him with great interest. "The bet allows seven."

The little man wiped his nose with the back of his hand.

"I reckon six air 'nuff," was all he said.

Then he slowly raised to a level the rifle, which was longer than himself, paused an instant, steady as a rock, and fired.

The clap of the bullet on the nail was heard, and a shout came from beyond:

"Druv through the board. Made a hole."

Without a word the little man took from his mouth a second bullet, put it on his hand, and reloaded with great rapidity.

The second shot made a dull thud.

The third, fourth, fifth and sixth were inaudible.

At the sixth shot, a clapping of hands came from the target, and a cheer spread from one side of the green to the other. The stakeholder marched up to the target, followed by an excited crowd, and discovered that the almost incredible feat had really been performed. The little man's first bullet had driven a hole through the board and into the tree; and the other bullets had piled themselves one on the other without touching the wood.

Jake Rhett pocketed the stakes, put his tongue in his cheek and squeaked out:

"Bet any man in this crowd twenty-five dollars, I put ten balls aout of a dozen in the same ho-el, and I've got the dockyments."

VIII

THE IMITATORS

It has been suggested that "The Novelette," first published in Boston by Ballou, in 1857, may have given Mr.

New Series, No. 219.

Old Series No. 540.

BEADLE'S

NEW DIME NOVELS

Westward Bound.

(See page 261)

Beadle — or Mr. Victor — the idea for the dime novels.[1]
However that may be, the success of the Beadle publications — five millions of them selling in the first four
years — made a number of publishers decide to give
Beadle and Adams their sincerest flattery.

Elliott, Thomes and Talbot of Boston were early in
the game. They are credited with making a start in
1864 or '65, but one of the few of their books which I
have seen was copyrighted, at any rate, in 1863. This is
"The Bravo's Secret; or, The Spy of the Ten. A Venetian
Tale." By Sylvanus Cobb, Jr. It seems to be Number 3
of their "Ten Cent Novelettes," which follow the
Beadles in size, but not in appearance. They had the
decency not to use the yellow covers.

In it is an advertisement of their "Brilliant Novelettes" at twenty cents each, including other titles by
Cobb; by "Ned Buntline," a Beadle author; and by Ben
Perley Poore — the newspaper correspondent, whose
venerable and distinguished figure is one of my earliest
recollections. It is a surprise to learn that he was the author of "The Scout; or, Sharpshooters of the Revolution."

Robert M. DeWitt, of Number 13 Frankfort Street,

---

[1] I have seen a "Novelette": it sold for more than a dime and its
appearance would not convict Mr. Beadle of slavish imitation.

New York, decided to make "DeWitt's Ten Cent Romances" look as much like their models as possible. He issued them in the same tint of orange paper, but had a design of ten copper cents at the top of the cover, above the picture, instead of the dime which appeared on many of the Beadles.

They began in 1867 and appeared once a month. The titles suggest Western and frontier adventure. The one before me is "The Mountain Trapper; or, The Ranger and the Bear." By Lieut. Henry L. Boone.

Among other early series of novels at ten cents are "Richmond's Novels," which were appearing in the eighteen seventies from the firm of Richmond and Company of Boston.

The story of Mr. Beadle's most formidable rival is rather odd. Mr. Edward S. Ellis wrote:

One day, when chatting with Mr. Beadle, he nodded toward the door leading to an outer room, in which an employee was tying up bundles of novels for shipment.

"There," said he, "is an illustration of the advantage of the English system over ours. That man has worked for us nearly two years. I pay him sixteen dollars a week; he is perfectly content with that; he will never wish to change his situation or try to improve it. If he were an American, he would speedily demand higher pay. As it is, he will be satisfied to grow old and serve us for the rest of his life."

The man, Mr. Ellis explained, was George P. Munro, a native of Nova Scotia, an industrious workman, who gave complete satisfaction to his employer. The latter had misjudged Munro's talent for advancement. He left the Beadles in 1866, or about one year after Mr. Beadle predicted his eternal docility and contentment. He joined partnership with Irwin Beadle and started the publication of the "New Dime Novels" with Irwin Beadle's name on the cover. This was rather too close for comfort; and Erastus Beadle stopped it by an injunction.

The title was then changed to "Munro's Ten Cent Novels." I have one here: it is printed on very cheap paper and is called "The Patriot Highwayman; A Tale of the Revolution." By the author of "Leah, the Forsaken." It was copyrighted in 1870, and is the third of a series which already numbered 163. The publisher was at Number 118 William Street; one of Beadle's old addresses.

His competition was alarming, and he compelled his former employer to cheapen the tone of his own books and deal more or less in blood and thunder, just as the yellow journalist stampedes the decent newspapers. His firm, years afterwards, published two of the most famous series of detective stories in American fiction: "Old Cap Collier" and "Old Sleuth."

When the contented Nova Scotian, the wrapper-up of bundles, died thirty years afterwards, it was not with a modest fortune like Mr. Beadle's; merely two or three millions. He had, so it is said, the princely sum of ten millions.

IX

A PERSONAL INTERLUDE

At recess the news had gone round the school — at least, among the boys. Bert Blake had run away! He had taken merely his 22-caliber revolver and the contents of his iron bank — probably $1.85 — and his own place knew him no more.

This was the most astonishing news heard in the Kelley School for at least a year. Running away from home was not our custom. Such bold strokes were done by the other boys: we read about it in the newspapers once in a while. We committed some of the traditional offences; we hooked apples in the apple season and un-hooked gates at Hallowe'en, and made ourselves mildly annoying at various times. But the large and gaudy sins were far beyond us.

We read about and admired Tom Bailey and his crew at Rivermouth, who exploded a whole battery of guns one night. And life in a cave, or on a raft, with piratical exploits, as carried out by Tom Sawyer and Huck Finn, were things distant and beautiful — like the lives of the saints.

Yet Bert had taken the bold step. Harry Waters' eyes bulged as he revealed his information:

"Mr. Blake's gone after him. They say he's going West to fight Indians."

"Who? Mr. Blake?" asked Roy McRae.

"No! Don't be a fool. Bert, of course. His mother thinks he must have been readin' dime novels!"

This astonished us all. Fred Upton suggested that Bert would be terrified by the smallest Indian, and George Spaulding observed that it was only a plot to stay away from school — an idea that struck most of us as particularly sage.

At all events, the matter remained a mystery for nearly two days — so long, in fact, that we almost forgot

Bert, and thought of him only as a bright memory of youth.

The news of the flight came on Monday morning. On Wednesday, Mr. Smith and Miss Short, who had the discipline of the school in their care, informed us that the wanderer had returned; the ex-Indian fighter would be in his accustomed seat at the afternoon session. One of them added:

"Now, Bert has been a very foolish boy; but he's sorry for it, and you are not, any of you, to talk to him about what he did."

Sure enough, that afternoon, there he was; a little pale, but otherwise as in former years. His scalp was in place, we were glad to notice. He had a slightly distant look in his eyes, as one who had beheld the towers of Cathay, but we could see nothing else wrong with him.

Mr. Blake, we learned, had overtaken him at the farthest point west which he had reached: Lynn, Massachusetts. He had no Indian trophies, nor was there any talk of buffaloes slain.

As soon as I got a chance, I spoke to Bert, and as cautiously as I could brought the talk around to dime novels. Not greatly to my surprise — for I knew Bert — he said he had never read one of them in his life. He didn't care for reading at all. Literature, nevertheless, was the curse of his existence, he told me, and it was directly due to the poisonous influence of four or five books that he had taken the desperate step which had alarmed his father and caused his mother to weep. He named those detestable works, and they were, in order of malignancy:

1. Harper's School Geography.
2. Ginn & Company's Reader.
3. Colburn's Arithmetic.
4. Somebody's Speller — a small, blue book.

This seemed to us all, as soon as we discussed it, a most important fact, which ought to be laid before the proper authorities. Here were four books which had directly impelled Bert into sin, had distressed his parents, and threatened the *morale* of his classmates. Ergo, they were improper and immoral books and should be cast out, if not burned in public.

None of the elders seemed aware of it; instead, they were really forcing these books on our attention. We thought of speaking to Master Lunt, the school superintendent, when he came on his next visit, but volunteers being called for, nobody had the courage.

The incident made a number of us reflect upon literary and ethical subjects. Why, for example, was Captain Mayne Reid's "Rifle Rangers" a righteous and proper book, when bound in board covers and borrowed from Miss Cary's circulating library, but a trap for the young when bound in paper and bought at Steve Fowle's newsstand for ten cents? What was it that caused Edward S. Ellis's "The Riflemen of the Miami" to be pure when it came from the shelves of the public library, or the Sunday-school library, but suddenly a well of poison and lair of serpents when bought — rather cleaner in condition — at the emporium of A. Parke Lewis?

To be sure, the question was complicated when some adult person pointed out that Mr. Lewis also sold tobacco and that he had a room where men smoked and played pool, and that boys who bought books in the front of the shop might some day be led into the dissipations which were rampant in the rear of it. But this begged the literary question and it remained unanswered.

X

MORALS, MORALS

HAD we known it, these questions were raised and answered and raised again, long before we were born.

The sale of dime novels by the million was such an astonishing event, in Civil War days, that it attracted the attention of the grave *North American Review,* and this Boston publication, in July, 1864, printed a review of "Beadle's Dime Books" which was written by William Everett. It was a conscientious attempt to recognize their merits, to point out their defects and understand their popularity.

Mr. Everett discussed the songbooks, the letter-writers, the biographies and other publications of the house. When he came to the novels, he said that he had read ten of them and that it was uphill work.

"Malaeska," by Mrs. Stephens, he thought was silly; "Alice Wilde," by Mrs. Victor, was better, although both books had defects in grammar. "Maum Guinea" was dismissed as merely one of the thousand stories derived from "Uncle Tom's Cabin." Edward S. Ellis's "Seth Jones" and "The Trail-hunters" were "good, very good." His Indians were human beings.

The novels as a whole, he found, were "unobjectionable morally, whatever fault be found with their literary style and composition. They do not even obscurely pander to vice, or excite the passions." He ended by wishing the Messrs. Beadle success.

This commendation naturally pleased the Messrs. Beadle, and they quoted it in their advertisements and in conversation for years thereafter. Its clean bill of health on moral grounds was exactly what they wanted, and they realized its commercial value.

The attacks on dime novels continued, however, and grew in strength. In the eighteen eighties, when the literary quality of the stories had cheapened, when hacks were turning out novels at lightning speed, and the pictures on the front covers heaped horrors on horror's head, there was justification for the assault. Cheap and cheaply sensational the books were; "immoral" they still were not and never became, if, by immoral, one means inciting to vice.

A boy who had been up to deviltry; parents who had shamefully neglected a son and allowed him to stray into mischief — say, a little highway robbery — these folk found it very convenient to stand in a police court and lay all the blame on dime novels. Inherent deviltry; neglect; selfishness; cruel egotism — oh, dear no. It was nothing but wicked dime novels. Willy was such a good boy until he began to read them. And, as not one of these grown-up persons looked at one of the novels, and discovered that if Willy had really been reading a dime novel at all, it may have been one of the Sunday-school type like "Honest Harry," or some Western tale, in which virtue was extolled and richly rewarded, this plea had great success.

Judges and teachers and clergymen and Sunday-school superintendents and even police chiefs began to denounce dime novels. It was the most useful explanation of crime, and the easiest excuse for the offender, until its place was taken by the cigarette, and then by the moving pictures. Finally, we achieved the psychosis, the inhibition, the slave phantasy, the fixation and the pituitary gland, and at last think that there are no more evil-doers — at least, not in the prisoner's dock or in jail. The prosecuting attorney may be a villain and the judge is probably a scoundrel. But nobody else.

When the notorious trial took place, in 1874, of Jesse Pomeroy, the sadistic murderer, it was suggested that Pomeroy might have been prompted to his offences by cheap "literature of the dime novel type." But Pomeroy spiked this, by telling the police that he had never read dime novels — nor about murder cases. Pomeroy is still in prison — the amiable attempts to have him released, which are analogous to an effort to scatter disease germs in a schoolroom, having failed — and the literature which he produces for the prison magazine is unexceptionable in moral tone.

Another murderer, named Piper, at about the same time, and in the same city (Boston) did try to suggest that his reading was not what it ought to have been. But the book he named turned out to be a novel published by a respectable house, and priced at $1.50.

It has been intimated, by the friends of the Beadles, that the more conservative and dignified publishers in New York, those who charged the conventional price for a novel, had no objections whatever to the widest circulation of the report that ten cent novels were vicious. I have never seen the slightest evidence, however, that these publishers did anything to further the belief.

An editorial attack on dime novels was made by the *New York Tribune*, in 1884. The specification in the charge was that three more boys had robbed their parents and "started off for the boundless West," and all through the influence of the usual kind of book. To this, Captain Frederick Whittaker, from his home in Mt. Vernon, New York, made a long and well-reasoned reply, as an old writer of dime novels. The *Tribune* duly printed it.[1] The arguments on both sides are familiar and need not

[1] March 16, 1884.

be reiterated. One of Captain Whittaker's lines of defence, although appealing strongly to writers, seems beside the ethical point which had been raised. It was that the house of Beadle had kept many authors from starvation. He cited their experience with Bret Harte — which had always been a thorn in the sides of Mr. Victor and Mr. Beadle. This is the passage:

The brilliant but erratic Bret Harte was in negotiation with the same house for the story of "Gabriel Conroy," and went over to the Scribners at the last moment, because they took the work on his reputation, without examination. Had he kept his engagement with the house that first ordered that work, it would never have been allowed to appear, till it had been properly written, from beginning to end. As it is, he is not living on literature, but on the public service, like Herman Melville, Nathaniel Hawthorne, Payne, and others before him.

The Beadles used frequently to reprint, in their weekly paper, the rules they sent to their authors:

Our Literature

So much is said, and justly said against a considerable number of papers and libraries now on the market, that we beg leave to call the attention of the public to the following circular, which we send to all who propose to write for any of our publications:

Authors who write for our consideration will bear in mind that

We prohibit all things offensive to good taste, in expression or incident —

We prohibit subjects or characters that carry an immoral *taint* —

We prohibit the repetition of any occurrence, which, though true, is yet better untold —

We prohibit what cannot be read with satisfaction by every right-minded person — old and young alike —

We require your best work —

We require unquestioned originality —

We require pronounced strength of plot and high dramatic interest of story —

We require grace and precision of narrative style, and correctness in composition.

Authors must be familiar with characters and places which they introduce, nor attempt to write in fields of which they have no intimate knowledge.

Those who fail to reach the standard here indicated cannot write acceptably for our several Libraries, or for any of our publications.

Others of their manifestoes appeared from time to time, in which they disclaimed responsibility for the "mischief that may have been, or yet, may be brought by certain other 'ten-cent' publications," (a salute to the former wrapper of bundles at sixteen dollars per week) and assuring the public that their own books were free from impurity of every kind.

The New York correspondent of the *Boston Evening Transcript*[1] became interested and wrote a long discussion of the controversy, in which he found that Captain Whittaker and the Beadles had a good case. He thought that the Western stories of adventure were harmless, but that the weekly papers of New York were sickening. He denounced the stories which made heroes out of Jesse James and other bandits. Then he wrote:

I went down into William Street the other day and made a visit to the father of the dime novel — Erastus F. Beadle. I climbed up the stairs, expecting to be stopped on every landing and to be asked for the countersign; but, to my surprise, the office was much like any other. There were no rifles in the corner, no scalps that I could see, no "keen, shining blades," no "haunch of venison" — nothing, alas! but the skin of some little animal that was stretched over a frame in the office of the editor. This was the only thing in the rooms that smacked of the "plains," and this, I am afraid, came from a Jersey swamp. The head of the house, Mr. Beadle, is an active, pleasant, white-bearded gentleman, a little

[1] March 27, 1884.

past the prime of life, who received me cordially, and told me quite an interesting story about the origin and development of the dime novel.

"The idea," said he, "occurred to me in '59, and I began publishing in '60. The state of the book market then was peculiar. Every one was publishing books with thick paper and wide margins — trying to see how little they could give their readers for a dollar or a dollar and a half. Publishers exchanged books, and took back such as were not sold. Well, I took the other tack, and thought I would see how much I could give for ten cents; cash sales, no credit. Every one said the project would fail, but it didn't. We first published dime song-books, cook-books, etiquette books, etc., which we bound in a salmon-colored cover. No 'yellow-covered dimes' were ever sent out by me; the color is salmon. The yellow-covered ones were imitations, and were a bad lot. Here is Mr. Victor, an old friend of Horace Greeley, my editor for many years; he knows more about these things than I do."

Mr. Victor took up the thread of the narrative and went on as follows:

"Our authors are well-known men. There's a book by a man who was once a member of the Ohio Legislature: another by an ex-governor of Ohio. He never wrote a bad line. Edward S. Ellis — you know him — wrote us our most popular novel. He was a Methodist, and he went to his minister to know whether he could write a dime novel."

"You see," continued the editor, "these novels introduced either historical or local characters. They followed right after 'Cooper's Tales,' which suggested them. Mrs. A. M. Dennison wrote historic fiction; Judge Jared Hall of Ohio wrote 'The Slave Sculptor,' a story of Montezuma's time — good names. Then there was Clara Augusta; you know her, of course. She is a Maine lady. Don't know her? Well, that doesn't speak very well for Boston culture. She's a famous writer." [This was very humiliating, but I had to bear up under the genial editor's reproaches and defended Boston as well as I could.] "Our stories were very popular and our rivals of the yellow covers and the Claude Duval series — bad books — began to spring up. What did we do then? Oh, we had to kill a few more Indians than we used to; we held our own against them. But ours are stories of exciting adventure only; there's nothing bad about them. See this article in the *North American Review* for July, 1864, wherein they are described and criticised. They are pronounced 'exceptionally moral,' and they 'do not even obscurely pander to vice or excite passions.' "

A sane view of the novels was expressed a few years later in *Lend a Hand*,[1] a magazine edited by the Reverend Edward Everett Hale.

William McCormick wrote in this magazine about "The Dime Novel Nuisance." He believed that the

[1] April, 1890.

novels *had* created runaway school boys, juvenile house--
breakers, and baby bandits. But, he added refreshingly,
exactly as false views of life come from the Sunday-
school library books.

"I have no patience," he said, "with the all-too-common
philanthropy that would rob the dirty-faced urchin of
his 'Bald-eagle Bob, the Boy Buccaneer,' and offer in
its stead, 'Willie Russell's Sacrifice.'

He preferred boys who had the intellectual curiosity,
such as it was, to read dime novels, to those who were
too dull to read at all. His plan was for exciting and
interesting books which were good in a literary and
ethical sense.

In his later years, Edward S. Ellis wrote an introduc-
tion for a new edition of "Seth Jones." He began with a
delicious story, which not only put the case for the dime
novel but also illustrated the militant attitude of the novelist himself, and his publishers, toward really "corrupting" stories, which were "French through and through."

Mr. Ellis wrote:

A goodly number of years ago, when I was connected
with a leading Sunday-school, in one of our prominent
cities, I noticed that a certain book in the library was
in constant demand among the pupils, especially by the

larger girls. It was in such favor that several copies would no more than have supplied the call for it. After a time I got hold of one copy and read it. No volume in the Sunday-school library was bound so handsomely, and it contained several artistic illustrations. The book was a French novel, and the first chapter was devoted to an account of an intrigue between a married woman and her lover. The entire work was French through and through. The sanctity of the marriage relation was jeered, and the story of one illicit amour after another was set forth in the most suggestive language. There could be no more corrupting work put in the hand of either sex. The poisonous seeds which it had already sown among the youths of the Sunday-school must have produced a frightful harvest.

Mr. Ellis takes this frightful harvest on trust — exactly like the opponents of dime novels.

He continues:

The superintendent of the school was an intelligent business man, held in the highest respect throughout the city. He was so occupied with his own duties throughout the week that he found no time to read anything of a secular nature, except the daily newspapers. I placed the volume referred to in his hands and asked him to examine it and to give me his views regarding it. He did so. When I saw him a week later he was pale with indignation.

"I am horrified," he said. "That vile work was read by my daughter only a short time ago. I never dreamed that such a serpent could creep into our library."

"How was it," I asked, "that it gained an entrance?"

"We appointed a committee last year to select new books for the library. Not one of the brethren was fitted for the task. They noticed that these 'Memoirs' were beautifully bound and had attractive pictures; that was enough for them, and no doubt that was the only test they used in making their selections. This particular pest, however, will do no more harm."

"Why not?"

"I have burned it, and shall make sure that it is never replaced. I shall give the next few weeks to a critical examination of the library, with special attention to the most popular books."

"Since you are going to take up the work of censor, will you oblige me by reading this little volume and tell me whether it is worthy of a place in the library?"

The superintendent smilingly took the work, which was neatly bound and printed, and assured me that he would do as I requested him to do. When he finished his perusal, some days later, he said, with a glowing face:

"If you will get me several copies of the book, I will put them in the library. I have never been more interested in a story; it is strong, stirring, and appeals to that love of incident and adventure which is natural to every healthy youth."

"But what of its moral tone?"

"It is *clean*. It does not contain a single evil thought; its tendency is in the right direction, and it leaves a pleasant taste in the mouth. I consider it the right kind of literature to put in the hands of the young."

"And yet that little book is a dime novel. I merely took off the paper cover and had it tastefully bound. You have given it the only true and fair test, and your verdict is what I expected to hear."

The superintendent was astonished, and could hardly credit what I had told him.

"Perhaps," he remarked quizzically, "the fact that I noticed it was written by you prejudiced me in its favor."

"More likely the prejudice worked the other way, but what you have said is another of the many proofs of the unthinking judgment of the multitude, based wholly upon appearances. The good brethren who gave that vicious French novel a prominent place in the Sunday-school library would have revolted at the proposal to put this little story beside it, for the reason that it has a paper cover, is of a salmon color, and is honest enough to proclaim the truth — that is, that it is a novel."

The above incident illustrates the prejudice that grew up and kept pace with the popularity of the original dime novel. At the same time, it cannot be denied that the disfavor of those publications became justified after a time.

XI

BEADLE'S AUTHORS

A LIST of "some of" Beadle's contributors which I have seen gives over two hundred and fifty names. This includes writers for the weekly paper and also more than a few pseudonyms and other duplications. Never were more tricks played with pen names; seldom have there been times when one writer was so apt to use three or four names, or when half a dozen would share a single *alias,* as in the golden days of the dime novel.

This was not literary coyness: there was usually a sound business reason. Some of the most famous characters and authors were trade names for a syndicate.

After most of the names in this list is the single word — "Dead." After a rather large number of them is the entry — "Suicide." And after a few is the explanation "Dead. Whiskey." There is a tragic element in the history of these authors, and a solemn warning to the young gentleman who considers adopting the profession of letters.

[104]

Many of them bore military or naval titles: lieutenants and ensigns, captains, majors and colonels. There were doctors and professors, and more than a few clergymen, including one of the writers of verse whom I remember as a very human and agreeable parson — Eben E. Rexford. There was Jack Clermont, who is briefly described as "a woman"; and another, about whom his fellow authors disputed not only as to his sex, but as to his race, color, and previous condition of servitude.

Some of the most popular of the Wild West stories were written by authors whose nearest acquaintance with the great plains was in White Plains, New York; while the most effective unmasking of the sin and sorrow of the metropolis, the most realistic exposé of the hollow life of millionaires in Fifth Avenue, came from men who had traveled not more than a hundred miles from their home in some small town of Kansas.

A few of the staff, wrote Mr. George C. Jenks, were good for one thousand words per hour, and they could keep it up, completing a seventy-thousand-word novel in a week. When typewriters came in, they became even speedier.

As an example of the man of action, take Colonel

Prentiss Ingraham, described as Beadle's most prolific author. This was a distinction to which no one need aspire until his number of novels had gone into the hundreds. Colonel Ingraham wore a slouch hat and a drooping white moustache; he was of the "Southern Colonel" type, and his appearance was a true index to his career.

He fought for the Confederacy, and when the War was over, it proved that no Northern government was strong enough to reconstruct him. He went south, and fought under Juarez in Mexico; east, and battled with Austria against Prussia in 1866; south again, and helped in Crete against the Turks. Some of these campaigns must have been brief — as indeed the one was between Austria and Prussia. Then he fought in Africa, and some say in Asia — quite in the manner of the soldiers of fortune about whom Richard Harding Davis used to write. He was in the Cuban "ten years' war" for independence — probably not the whole of it. He was a captain in the Cuban navy and a colonel of cavalry in their army. The Spaniards caught him and sentenced him to death, but when the wall and the firing squad were ready, they couldn't find the Colonel. He came back to America, and was with Buffalo Bill in the

West — he probably wrote most of the stories signed by that great hunter.

His literary career began in 1870, and it resulted in the publication of more than six hundred novels, as well as plays and short stories. He had also found time to study medicine at some period in his career.[1]

On one occasion he wrote a thirty-five-thousand-word novel in a day and night. He locked himself in with a fountain pen and reams of paper, and wrote from breakfast to breakfast.

"I was both tired and hungry when I finished," remarked the Colonel; "for I had had only a sandwich or two, eaten as I worked."

Contrast this giant with the mild-looking and soft-spoken Edward L. Wheeler, who was nevertheless the creator and chief author of the most famous of the desperadoes, "Deadwood Dick." Mr. Wheeler is said to have called everybody "pard," but it was merely an esthetic mannerism, for there is a rumor that he was never in his life farther west than Jersey City.

Major Sam S. Hall, or "Buckskin Sam," was really himself a frontier boy. He wrote a story whose title has always delighted me: "Double Dan, the Dastard; or,

[1] See obituary notice in the *Bookman* (New York), October, 1904.

The Pirates of the Pecos." He also celebrated a famous hero of Texas: "Big-Foot Wallace, The King of The Lariat; or, Wild Wolf, The Waco." Another of his stories was "Ker-whoop, ker-whoo!; or, The Tarantula of Taos."

Major Hall, says a caustic writer (Mr. James M. Cain), "occasionally showed his virile Western manhood by going on a shooting rampage at his home in Wilmington, Delaware." He was a wiry little man, whose grammar needed careful supervision by Mr. Victor.

He rather shocked even Beadle and Adams by his "Giant George, The Ang'l of the Range. A Tale of Sardine-Box City, Arizona." (I cannot explain why the "e" is omitted from Angel, but so it is.) The picture on the cover showed Giant George giving his burro, Don Diablo, a drink of whisky — and this exceeded the usual license allowed to authors or artists. The hero's language was deep purple:

"Hoop-La! Set 'em up! Sling out yer p'ison before I stampede through yer hull business! I'm ther 'Bald-headed Eagle o' ther Rockies,' an' are a-huntin' sum galoot what's got ther sand ter stomp on my tail-feathers. Shove out a bar'l o' bug-juice afore I bu'st up yer shebang; fer my feed-trough are chuck full o' cobwebs, an' as dusty as Chalk Canyon. Hoop-la! Don't be bashful, Don Diablo! Don't you go fer ter go back on yer raisin'. Show all ther brass an' grit yer has got in yer karkiss. An' yer needn't try ter shake up vim enuff ter stampede outen this, for yer hain't got ther muscle arter our long trail ter kick over a cotton-tail'd rabbit. Glide this-a-ways, an' we'll pour down a small decoction o' chain-lightnin' what'll make us feel kinder nat'ral-like."

The speaker, as he shouted the first expressions that commence our story, stepped into one of the many hastily-constructed bar-rooms of Sardine-Box City, Arizona, holding in his hand a lariat which was drawn taut.

One instant his eyes darted glances around the bar, and then he turned about, continuing as recorded, by addressing himself apparently to some person outside who seemed reluctant to enter.

As may be supposed, those in the bar-room were greatly astonished, not only at the words, but also at the manner and appearance of the stranger, as well as from the fact that he had seemingly gotten his lariat attached to someone who was being dragged about against his will.

All this was soon explained, for as the bar-room loungers gazed open-mouthed, the newcomer gave a powerful pull at the rope, leaning his heavy weight upon it, brought round his hips as it was for the purpose, and the next instant a most comical-looking burro, its huge, snuff-colored ears lying viciously along its neck, shot inside the door. This sudden movement slackened the lariat so quickly that the owner of the animal fell to the floor with a shock that shook the building.

Quickly rising to a sitting posture, the "Bald-headed Eagle of the Rockies," as he had proclaimed himself, gazed into the face of the burro which stood in the middle of the floor looking as innocent as a lamb.

"Waal, dod blast yer pecul'ar pictur', Don Diablo, I wouldn't 'a' thunk yer'd 'a' gone back on me, er knocked ther props from under me thet-a-ways. I wouldn't 'a' thunk yer'd 'a' made a spread eagle o' yer old pard, an' I'm dog-gon'd good mind ter drink alone. I've stood by yer 'mong 'Pache yells, dry cricks, an' close feed, an' now ye're tryin' ter disgrace me! Who's thet laff'd?" he continued, springing to his feet, and drawing a huge bowie-knife. "I kin carve ther nose offen ther galoot thet laffs at me er Don Diablo. I kin shoot ther eyelids offen the cuss what smiles. I kin dissect ther in'ards o' ther pilgrim or tender-hoof what looks crossways or puckers a lip at me or my outfit, fer I'm plum full an' b'ilin over with hydrophobic!"

Turning about, the speaker raised his bowie and, bringing his hand down suddenly, buried the point of the blade in the pine plank that served as a counter.

"Hoop-la! Did yer hear me whisper whiskey? Dig ther bugs outen yer ears an' trot it out quicker'n an alligator gar kin skute, or I'll make toothpicks outen the hull caboodle!"

BEADLE'S
Dime
New York Library

COPYRIGHTED IN 1879, BY BEADLE & ADAMS.

Vol. VI. Published Every Two Weeks. *Beadle & Adams, Publishers,* 98 WILLIAM STREET, N. Y., July 2d, 1879. Ten Cents a Copy. $2.50 a Year. No. 71

CAPTAIN COOL BLADE; or, THE MAN-SHARK OF THE MISSISSIPPI.

BY JOSEPH E. BADGER, Jr.,

AUTHOR OF "THREE-FINGERED JACK," "GOSPEL GEORGE," "THE BOY JOCKEY," ETC., ETC.

"TAKE ONE STEP FORWARD, JACQUES BOUCHIER, AND, BY THE HORN OF GABRIEL! I'LL SCATTER YOUR BRAINS TO THE FOUR WINDS!"

"TAKE ONE STEP FORWARD, JACQUES BOUCHIER,
AND, BY THE HORN OF GABRIEL! I'LL SCATTER
YOUR BRAINS TO THE FOUR WINDS!"

(See page 268)

This skill in language recalls the raftsmen of the Mississippi who were overheard by Huckleberry Finn.[1] In "Mustang Sam, The King of the Plains," by Joseph E. Badger, there is a speech on the same high plane:

"You ax who I be. I'm Mustang Sam, the *high muck-a-muck* of E. Pluribus Unum. I was got by a bull whale out o' a iceberg. I kin yell louder, run furder, ride faster, shoot straighter, jump higher, tell bigger lies, eat more poor bull, an' jump outside o' more chain-lightnin' than any other two-legged critter as was ever pupped. I'm the man what swum up the Big Kenyon of the Colorado on my back. I'm the critter what climbed up a greased rainbow an' bit the highest p'int off o' the new moon. I'm Mustang Sam — how goes it, stranger?"

Badger was another prolific author, with scores of novels to his credit. He was also a man of the frontier and ended his life in Kansas. He wrote his own life, calling it "Roving Joe," and signing it "A. H. Post." He could not only write picturesque speech but also describe a good fight. Here is the climax of his "Old Bull's Eye, the Lightning Shot of the Plains."

The recognition was mutual. Old Bull's Eye saw before him the man who had wronged him so terribly

---

[1] In the passage left out of his own history, and included in Chapter III of "Life on the Mississippi."

— who had made him an outcast and wanderer upon the face of the earth — the man whom he had sought through so many long, weary years.

"At last, Antone Barillo — at last!"

The words sounded like a death-knell. With a low, inarticulate cry, the wretched ranchero strove to arise, but then he fell back, his face livid, a bloody froth gathering upon his lips. It seemed as though the hand of death was upon him.

Old Bull's Eye dropped the torch and bent forward, his face white with a terrible hatred.

"Antone Barillo — thief, murderer! where are my wife and child? Speak, or by the God above! I will tear your false heart out with my naked hands! Speak — "

"Kinder easy, pard," interposed Jack Hardy, laying one hand upon the maddened man's shoulder. "Don't you see — "

With a howl of fury, Old Bull's Eye whirled around and dealt the tall Texan a terrible blow full in the face, that hurled him headlong into one of the fires, where he lay, quivering and bleeding like a stuck pig.

Instantly a yell of anger arose, and the men sprung forward to avenge their comrade, though not comprehending what the sudden fracas was about. Hardy rolled out of the fire, and staggering to his feet, gazed bewilderingly around.

Old Bull's Eye saw the crowd springing toward him, and it seemed to set him wild. Drawing his pistols, he discharged them in rapid succession, yelling and cursing like a very fiend. And now his widespread celebrity stood him in good stead, for the entire party seemed afraid to close upon him, so long as he held those terrible weapons in his hands.

Jack Hardy brushed the mingled blood and ashes from his eyes, and then catching sight of Old Bull's Eye, whipped forth a huge knife and staggered forward. As the scout was busied with the enemy in front, he knew naught of his danger, and the glittering blade was already raised above his back, when a sharp report came from the outer circle, and the big Texan fell back, without a groan, a bullet-hole in his forehead.

The next instant a lithe figure flashed across the glade and stood before Old Bull's Eye. It was Carmela, her face aglow, a still smoking revolver clasped in her right hand. Her aim had saved the scout's life.

"Hold!" cried a loud, commanding voice. "You are surrounded — the man who lifts another weapon dies!"

Edward Zane Carroll Judson, who preferred to call himself "Ned Buntline," was another of the authors whose career seems almost mythical. Some of its details are accepted, however, by the biographical dictionaries, and he has been made the subject of a book.[1]

He was born in Philadelphia in 1822, and was writing for the *Knickerbocker Magazine* as early as 1838. Be-

[1] "The Life and Adventures of Ned Buntline." By Frederick E. Pond, 1919.

fore this, he ran away to sea; made a gallant rescue of some drowning people in New York harbor; and was given a midshipman's commission by President Van Buren. On board the *Levant* he fought seven duels with other midshipmen, who had refused to mess with him because he had been a common sailor. He escaped without injury; we do not hear about his opponents. In the Civil War, he was Chief of Scouts with the Indians, and received twenty wounds.

Before the war, however, he had been connected with the foundation of the Know Nothing Party and also took such a part in leading the mob in the Astor Place Riot that he spent a year (not uncomfortably) in jail, on Blackwell's Island. He was at this time editing a weekly called *Ned Buntline's Own*.

He enjoyed agitation and oratory and delivered vent speeches in the cause of total abstinence. Charles Sutton says that "in his palmy days he was a great favorite with the 'b'hoys'," which is a delicate way of intimating that Ned was not always an agitator for temperance. His income from literature, at one period, was reputed to be twenty thousand dollars annually.

Mr. Cain says that Judson and Buffalo Bill used to ride down Broadway, eight or ten times a day, wearing

full Western costume, and dismount impressively at
the door of their publisher. Their object was merely the
furtherance of sales of their books.

Ned Buntline's story of "Red Ralph, the Ranger; or,
The Brother's Revenge" goes back to Virginia of 1753,
and for characters, to the Rolfe family, only one generation removed from Pocahontas herself.

He opens with a sentence which is full of information.

It was a beautiful place, that of Edgar Rolfe, situated
upon the banks of the James river, chosen by his father,
when hand in hand he roamed through the forest with
the noble-hearted and queenly Pocahontas, whom he
married, and who died but too soon after she gave birth
to her only son — died a stranger in a foreign land,
but not unwept did she perish.

The tale concerns the sons of Edgar Rolfe: the elder
and wicked son, Francis, and the younger and noble
Eugene. The latter is in love with a young lady of
French descent — Migionette Minier, who was "all
tenderness, all love, all gentleness":

I said she was beautiful as the flower from which she
was named. Why should I compare female beauty to a
flower, unless, alas, that like the flower's loveliness, it
too must wither and fade away. If a form to which noth-

ing could be added or aught taken away without marring its perfection, if a face whose complexion was so transparent, so blended with the lily and the rose, that even the envious man could not tarnish its loveliness — if eyes darkly, beautifully blue and liquid as a violet's in the dewy-morn — if hair like sun-beams twisted into waving, golden curls, could constitute beauty, then was Migionette very beautiful.

The elder Rolfe informs Eugene that he can secure him a commission in His Majesty's army or navy. Eugene is not interested. As they talk together, in the park, a canoe passes along the river. In it are a youth and maiden: the Miniers, brother and sister.

Eugene arose, and walked down to the bank and hailed young Minier.

"Where away this sunny day, Gustave?" he cried.

"I am going with my sister up to the old settlement to gather some grapes, sir," replied young Minier in a full, manly voice. "They are ripe and very fine — will you not go along?"

"Not now — I may ride up there by and by," replied Eugene. "How is the fair Migionette to-day?"

"Well and happy!" cried a voice as sweet and soft as the tone of a flute heard at eve across the waters.

"She is very beautiful!" muttered the elder Rolfe to himself. "It must be as Francis says. This intimacy must be stopped before it goes too far! The blood of the Rolfes must not be contaminated!"

The canoe was soon out of sight in the deep shadows of the trees up the river, and Eugene returned to the side of his father.

"That Minier girl is very good looking," said the father, apparently in a careless manner, but his eye now noted the expression of his son's face.

"She is, and as good and virtuous as she is beautiful!" said the young man earnestly.

"Perhaps so," said the father in a sarcastic tone. "Female virtue, however, is like other fruit — it may seem fair to view outside, and still be rotten at the core."

"Sir!" cried the youth, first turning pale with anger and then flushing as red as carnation. "Sir, were any other man than my father so much as to hint that Migionette Minier was not as pure as a spotless lily of the lake, as free from sin in thought, word or deed as a babe but an hour old, I would strike him dead at my feet! This I expect is some further work of my attentive brother. He had better beware or he may make me forget that the same blood flows in our veins. Good day, sir — I cannot converse properly with one who for a moment will cherish an evil thought in regard to one whom I know to be spotless and innocent as an angel in heaven — one who is as pure and well descended as we are, whose only fault is that her parents are poor!"

The wicked brother and his minions are baffled and defeated throughout the novel, but the story ends,

[117]

nevertheless, in disaster and sorrow, with the slaughter of all the Miniers by Indians. Eugene is left swearing an oath of vengeance — perhaps an indication of a sequel.

Whether "Deadly-Eye" was really by the Honorable W. F. Cody (Buffalo Bill) as signed, or by his assistant, Colonel Prentiss Ingraham, a passage of it shall be quoted, if only as a small return for that thrilling moment, one evening in the year 1893, when, to my great delight, Buffalo Bill, on his white horse, rode into the arena at Chicago.

"Every man to his post."

It was the clear and commanding voice of the Unknown Scout that gave the order, and the effect upon the pioneers was electrical, while they felt that in him they had a leader who fully understood the cunning of the Indians, and whose bravery was upon every tongue on the frontier.

True, strange stories were told of the remarkable man, and the Indians and a few bordermen held the superstitious idea that he was leagued with the Evil One, for around his whole life hung a mystery, the curtain of which none could raise.

Frequently he had aided frontiersmen and also wagon-trains moving through the Indian country, and also had given warning to settlements of the coming of the red-skin and the Branded Brotherhood; but that he was looked upon by the military with some suspicion — was known to be on intimate terms with many Indian warriors and had often been seen in close vicinity to the stronghold of Ricardo and his cruel band, were acknowledged facts.

Still, the emigrants were glad that Deadly-Eye was with them, and his having just rescued from captivity two of their train, caused them to look most kindly upon him.

"Scout, you are well accustomed to scenes like this one about to be forced upon us, and I would like you to take command," cried Major Conrad, advancing quickly to the side of the Unknown Scout, who glanced out upon the prairie toward the coming Indians, as he replied:

"Fortunately the train is in *corral,* sir, and the men are ready for a fight. I would advise that the women and children be placed under cover of the river-bank yonder, and the ravine will also protect the horses and cattle, while, with the wagons for a breast-work, the men can hold out splendidly."

This advice was acted upon, and in a few moments the camp was ready for action.

Stationing himself upon the outer edge of the line of wagons, Deadly-Eye was seen to suddenly raise his repeating rifle; a quick air, a shout, and a painted warrior fell from his horse, and a yell of exultation from the emigrants was answered by a series of wild war-whoops from the infuriated Indians.

[119]

"Now, Major Conrad, you see that I knew yonder renegade guide well, for he is doubtless the leader of the approaching band of red-skins, and was guiding you into a trap," said the Unknown Scout.

"We have much to thank you for, sir; but the Indians have halted."

"Yes, they are too wary to charge these lines in the daytime, and — "

"And what, sir?" asked Major Conrad, as the Scout paused, thoughtfully.

"And by nightfall I can bring relief, for not many miles from here is a band of Pawnees hunting buffalo."

"But, sir, you can never escape from here, for see, the Indians are beginning to surround us, and two separate parties are swimming the river."

The Unknown Scout took in the scene at once, and then said, quietly:

"You must hold the red devils at bay. Mind, act only on the defensive, and I will run the gauntlet of their fire, and bring what relief I can."

A shrill whistle followed, and the steed of Deadly-Eye trotted up to his master, and stood ready for his command.

Remonstrance with the Scout was useless, for after another warning to all, he sprung into the saddle and rode down to the river.

A word of encouragement to Prairie Gull, and the noble animal bounded into the clear waters, and was soon swimming bravely toward the other shore, fol-

lowed by the eyes of all the emigrants, who were waft-
ing God-speed to the daring man periling his life to
aid them.

Ere half the river was crossed the Indians discovered
the Scout, and with discordant yells the two parties,
one up and the other down the stream, rushed to cut
him off ere he could escape.

The Scout observed their intention but kept bravely
on, urging his horse, however, to swim still faster.

Leading one of these parties who were rushing toward
the point where the Scout was to land, was the traitor
guide, Red Dick, who now seemed to feel assured that
his revenge would be satiated, for he urged his large
roan forward at a tremendous pace, quickly shooting
ahead of the inferior horses ridden by the red-skins.

Soon the Scout reached the other shore, and dis-
mounting, the horse shook himself like a huge New-
foundland dog.

Then the girths were tightened, and the holster pistols returned to their places; after which the Scout
mounted as coolly as though almost certain death did not
stare him in the face.

The deadly rifle was raised, and with a quick aim was
fired in the direction of the band farthest off. A red
brave threw up his arms and fell from his steed, to be
trampled upon by those behind.

Again the rifle rung out, and the large roan ridden
by Red Dick was seen to stagger, stumble, and then go
heavily down, hurling his giant rider with terrible force
upon the ground.

From the lips of Deadly-Eye then broke forth his wild and blood-stirring war-whoop of defiance, and away bounded Prairie Gull, keeping an equal distance between the two lines rushing furiously upon him and hardly more than two hundred yards distant.

"On, on, my good steed, for you have a brave duty to perform, and the bright eyes of beauty are upon you," cried Deadly-Eye, as he turned in his saddle, and glanced back toward the camp. Seeing the action the pioneers gave him three hearty cheers, which the Indians answered with their discordant yells.

"But, what is the daring rider going to do? Has his courage failed him? Is he mad?"

Such were the hurried questions that burst from the astonished emigrants' lips as they saw Deadly-Eye suddenly come to a halt, and coolly gaze first upon one side and then upon the other.

The name of Buffalo Bill recalls the fact that many real characters of the frontier appear in the Beadle novels. James Fenimore Cooper Adams, called "Bruin" Adams, wrote, in "Old Grizzly, the Bear-Tamer," some account of his uncle, an extraordinary person, with a peculiar name (James Capon Adams), who was born at Seneca Lake, New York, but is reputed to have gone about the frontier country mounted on a large grizzly bear, with a second bear as attendant.

Pocket Series
No. 241.

BEADLE'S

Illuminated.
Ten Cents.

POCKET NOVELS

ONE DIME

Old Grizzly.

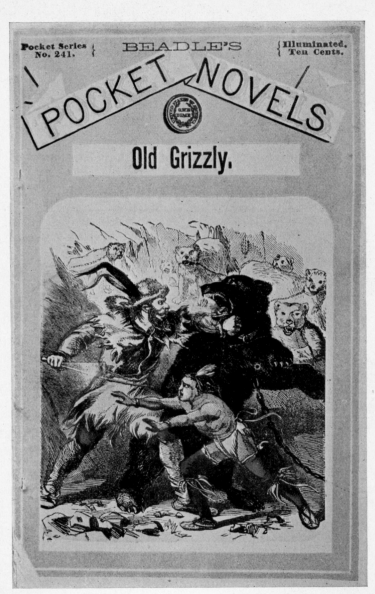

(See page 260)

Colonel Ingraham wrote "Texas Jack, The Mustang King," a novel founded on the adventures of the scout and hunter whose real name was J. B. Omohundro.

Kit Carson; Big Foot Wallace; Wild Bill Hickok; Captain Jack Crawford, the Poet Scout; General Custer; Arizona Joe Bruce; and Joaquin Marieta are men about whom sober accounts have been written. They had already figured, and at an early date, in these romantic biographies, in dime-novel form.

Another Beadle author, a man who produced novels by the score, was Albert W. Aiken, who came from a family of actors and writers. A queer-looking man, with a strangely elongated head, he sat in a little upper room at Number 98 William Street, writing with the regularity of a pendulum. He was high in favor with Mr. Victor, for the editor knew he could depend on a completed manuscript from him every Saturday night. His specialty was Western stories.

Charles Dunning Clark was one of the large number of newspaper men on the Beadle staff. His pseudonym as novelist was W. J. Hamilton. He died at Oswego in 1892, where he had been a local historian, and long a member of the staff of the Oswego *Times*. He wrote historical novels and Indian stories.

[123]

DIME NOVELS

Oll Coomes of Atlantic, Iowa, was killed by a motor car in 1920; one of his distinctions is the fact that almost alone among the dime novelists he invested his money with profit. He was a real son of the frontier and wrote about the country he knew. He does not seem to have tried to describe the dangers of Broadway.

A distinguished, amiable and rather pathetic figure was Thomas Chalmers Harbaugh, who might dispute with Colonel Ingraham in number of titles. Mr. Harbaugh was a Maryland man, who began to write in 1867. He usually lived in a small Ohio town, but the scenes of his novels covered the continent.

He was able to name thirty-seven volumes of fiction, poetry and local history, of which he was the author, all of them respectably bound in boards, and published toward the end of his life, when the Beadle days were past. And these were in addition to an endless number of dime novels. He wrote under several pseudonyms besides his own name, and is even credited, or charged, with writing some of the "Old Cap Colliers," and also some "Nick Carters."

Despite all this shocking drudgery, the newspapers recorded, in 1923, that he had sold his few possessions and entered the poorhouse at Casstown, Ohio. He was referred to in some of the head-lines as the "Dime Novel King." He died in the following year.

Because it was written by one of the few survivors of all this band, we should look at a short passage from "Lady Jaguar, The Robber Queen. A Romance of the Black Chaparral," by William H. Manning. It shows how they represented the vamp in 1882:|

He fixed his gaze upon the door, and, at the end of five minutes, Lady Jaguar entered with the grace peculiar to well-bred Spanish women.

She was clad in a plain but becoming costume, while a mask of unusual size concealed her whole face except the dark, handsome eyes, which he felt sure were in keeping with her whole face.

Edgar arose with the instinct of a gentleman, but she waved him back with her hand.

"Retain your seat, Don Edgar. If you would speedily recover from your wound, you must be discreet," she said, in the old, calm, deep voice.

"I am not so sure that I wish to recover if it be the means of sending me from here," he could not help saying.

"Gallantry, Don Edgar, is not for the chaparral and outlaws," was the cold reply, as the lady seated herself near him.

"Why do you call yourself an outlaw? Judged from my standpoint, you are — "

"An outlaw still," she interrupted, calmly. "But enough of this. I did not come to speak of myself. El Alacran said you were here and wounded, and I came at his bidding. I am sorry for you, but you will remember I warned you plainly."

"You did, and I owe all this to my own disobedience. El Alacran also gave me hope that you would explain how you came to know so much of me."

"You mistake. He said I would tell *what* I know of you, not how I gained my information."

"I accept the correction. Well, then, to open the field, what do you know of me?"

"You have heard of men who spend their lives in trying to create gold from baser metals?"

"Yes."

"Did one of them ever succeed?"

"Not that I am aware of."

"They are mad to try, but you are equally so to follow a shadow in the shape of a woman."

Probably, Edgar Lewis had never seen a more novel and perplexingly interesting moment in his life. To sit face to face with this masked and mysterious robber queen was strange in itself, but with all the other mysteries added it was doubly so. He felt sure she was young and handsome, but when, man-like, he would have indulged in gallantry, the uncertainty stifled the words and annoyed him. . . .

Edgar made one stride and caught the arm of Lady Jaguar in a remorseless grasp.

"Woman," he hissed, "beware what you say. I will not stand here tamely and hear you insult her. I tell you there is no crime at her door, and only your sex at this moment saves you from chastisement."

The robber queen shrunk under his touch and before his passion like a dying woman. Her strength seemed all gone, her breath came gaspingly, her bosom heaved, and only for his frenzy, Edgar would have been alarmed.

As it was, her emotion seemed to him more like the alarm of guilt, and he added:

"Who are you, anyway, who dares sit there and read my heart? I am tempted to tear that mask from your face!"

PART II

WILD DAYS

I

THE EIGHTEEN EIGHTIES

IN the summer of 1881, dime novels had attained their majority. Business was good. The factory on William Street, if not roaring, was steadily humming, and Mr. Beadle's fortune was being salted down.

Upstairs, his hacks were driving their pens across paper with the antlike persistence and clocklike punctuality of the author of "Barchester Towers." There was this difference: Anthony Trollope could work like a machine, and produce "The Last Chronicle," while all that poor Mr. Aiken could bring forth was "Old Benzine, The Hard Case Detective." But each delighted his publisher.

The editors had but to look over the manuscript and delete any excess of alcohol or approach to profanity. Then the printing presses, on another floor, took it up, and soon the story was being wrapped in bales and shipped to the news dealers of this and other lands.

All over the country, other authors, less visibly shackled and tied to the Beadle presses, were sending in shoals of manuscripts, stories and poems, for the dime-

[131]

novel series or the *Star Journal* — under whatever name that weekly might be appearing.

The competitors, especially Munro, were also doing very well indeed. The Beadles were having to "kill a few more Indians" to meet the competition. "A few more!" They had to kill them in droves. Mr. Ellis denounced the Munro novels as "absolute trash," and condemned Mr. Beadle for "seeing only the commercial side" and going about it to "degrade" his publications in order to meet his former clerk on his own ground.

To the American of 1881, the Civil War was but a few years farther back into the past than is the Great War to us of to-day. Men who had taken part in the war between the States, and who did not consider themselves exactly senile, found that they had to explain to smart youths that when they spoke of "the War," they did not mean the French and Indian War, or even the Revolution.

Slavery, and the old hostility between South and North, still flared up in Congress now and then, but it was already bad form to "wave the bloody shirt." Indeed, at an earlier election a Democrat had almost been elected to the presidency.[1]

[1] Democrats should amend this line to read: "had been duly elected and scandalously deprived of his rights by the Republicans."

BEADLE'S
Dime
New York Library

COPYRIGHTED IN 1880, BY BEADLE & ADAMS.

ENTERED AT THE POST OFFICE AT NEW YORK, N. Y., AS SECOND CLASS MAIL MATTER.

Vol. VIII. Published Every Two Weeks. *Beadle & Adams, Publishers,* 98 WILLIAM STREET, N. Y., May 5, 1880. Ten Cents a Copy. $2.50 a Year. No. 93

CAPTAIN DICK TALBOT,

KING OF THE ROAD;

Or, The Black-Hoods of Shasta.

BY ALBERT W. AIKEN,

AUTHOR OF "THE SPOTTER DETECTIVE," "THE NEW YORK SHARP," "OVERLAND KIT," "INJUN DICK," ETC, ETC.

"SHUT OFF STEAM OR YOU'RE A DEAD MAN!" THE LEADER CRIED, RIDING UP TO THE CAB AND "COVERING" THE ENGINEER WITH HIS WEAPON.

"SHUT OFF STEAM OR YOU'RE A DEAD MAN!"

THE EIGHTEEN EIGHTIES

The Republicans, as usual, were having too much success, and were beginning to quarrel. A vitriolic orator, Senator Conkling of New York, was especially bitter against the leader of his party, the new President, General Garfield of Ohio. The mighty question was: who should name the postmaster of New York? The nation was invited to become inflamed over this matter, but at the height of the dispute, the President was shot by a crank.

There followed three long and weary months; a painful illness for the wounded man, and at last his death on a night in September. At two o'clock the next morning, at his home on Lexington Avenue in New York, the vice president succeeded to the highest office. Among those present was Mr. Elihu Root.

This new President was Mr. Arthur, who had been a little distrusted as a mere "New York politician," but proved, instead, to be an honorable and dignified statesman. Indeed, his abilities are perhaps a little overestimated by those who feel that the liking for good clothes shown by Mr. Arthur, as well as his courtly manner, are the prime qualities needed in the White House.

There is a slight indication, at this period, of greater European influence upon America, and still more drift from the pioneer flavor of life in the sixties. The pallid-faced Americans, with bad digestions, are not so often mentioned. College athletics were far from unknown, and illustrated papers, like *Harper's Weekly,* carried pictures of large groups of people gathered to watch two young men play the game of lawn tennis. Small boys and muckers, however, always true conservatives, felt it their duty to denounce tennis as a pastime for sissies, or, even worse, for dudes.

One of the most dangerous social menaces of the time was the dude. Throughout the country, thousands of people religiously believed that up and down Fifth Avenue in New York, there was a perpetual parade of vacant-faced youths, made even more silly in appearance by single eyeglasses, and with the heads of large walking sticks thrust in their mouths. They wore absurd bell-crowned top hats, short monkey jackets, and tight trousers. If they ever took the walking stick out of their mouths during a walk, they held both arms in a curve, with elbows crooked. These were dudes.

Who could doubt their existence? They were pictured in *Puck* and *Life,* and had become so much a distinct type — like the comic Englishman, Dutchman or Irishman — that in Palmer Cox's "Brownies" in *St. Nicholas,* children always hunted for the Dude, as a beloved figure of fun. Dudes appeared in the dime novel, to the scorn of all real men, and one figured, in a not unfriendly light, in the novels of Archibald Clavering Gunter.

In far western regions, men are said to have become almost speechless with rage at these creatures, and even to have ridden twenty or thirty miles to meet a train reported to be carrying some "New York dudes." It is asserted that they muttered their threats to shoot these vermin on sight.

This may be an exaggeration. It is in my knowledge that the word "dude," applied in jest to a gardener and odd-job man, in a New England town, aroused him to such an access of fury that he used sometimes to pursue his tormentors with a sickle, in order to wipe out the insult in blood. To-day, the word and its meaning have vanished from the language, except in the localized term, "dude ranch."

The possibilities of a catchword, or a phrase, are similarly illustrated by the "New Woman" of 1894 and the "flapper" of the present decade. Everybody talked about them and felt their ominous influence — but nobody could point to a living specimen. Nevertheless, in the early nineties, sermons were preached against the "New Woman," who was about to break up the American home. Her equipment for doing this consisted of a bicycle and a pair of bloomers. The country editor, in New England, is sure of the existence of the "typical New Yorker" who never goes to bed, but lives in a perpetual round of night clubs; while even so intelligent a writer as Mr. Eugene O'Neill seems to think that the male population of Connecticut consists entirely of tight-lipped persons named Abner or Ezra, who say "purty" for "pretty," and are never so happy as when burning a witch.

In the 1880's, the eminent poets and editors of Lincoln's day had become venerable, gray-bearded gentlemen, the subjects for leisurely biographical sketches in *Harper's*. That magazine, in 1881, was publishing "A Laodicean," by Thomas Hardy. And *Harper's Weekly* was able to please its readers with a serial story by a novelist of world-wide fame. To-day hardly any one remembers this novelist, and nobody under forty could give the title of one of his books. He was William Black.

We jeeringly call the period the "elegant eighties." Full beards were going out, slowly, and side whiskers were in high favor — although their most celebrated expositor, General Ambrose E. Burnside, died that summer.

Hoop skirts were much reduced, but absurdity in woman's costume was more than compensated in other ways. Folk who deplore the good old times and become scandalized about the clothes worn by girls to-day, are invited to inspect the fashion plates of the eighties, when basques and flounces, bustles and bodices were correct, and when, instead of simple hats, women piled upon their heads the waving plumes of an ostrich, or the entire stuffed cadaver of a cock pheasant, or a poll parrot.

There was more freedom, and there was less. The characters in the story described a few pages farther along, could legitimately buy a glass of beer or a bottle of champagne. The men might not smoke in a drawing-room, as now, but the women might not smoke at all. The woman who chose to wear her hair short was apt to be mobbed. There were many taboos, but these had some justification. Girls in tights, on the stage, seemed amazingly wicked and alluring; but, on the other hand, no premium was put on stale wit and bad music as now, by the fact that the management could exhibit girls with almost no clothes at all. Novelists were forbidden to write about "sex" — although Mr. Hardy, the liberator, was arriving — but, on the other hand, third-rate novels did not get attention merely because they dwelt on the subject. "Hamlet" had to be expurgated, when produced, while now the expurgated lines are the first to be restored. But, while there was a mincing nicety of language, in 1881, some of our juvenilities were absent. No dramatist, for instance, glowed with boyish enthusiasm and wrote a whole scene to lead up to the moment when some commonplace word of Elizabethan times — like *bastard* — could be uttered openly on the stage.

II

THE DETECTIVES: OLD CAP

"NEW HAVEN, the beautiful City of Elms, was startled from its propriety and awakened to a sense of horror by a terrible announcement at half-past five o'clock on the morning of the 6th of August, 1881. Jennie E. Cramer, a comely young girl, was discovered in the water, face downward, DEAD!"

This is the first paragraph of a pamphlet called "The Beautiful Victim of the Elm City Tragedy" published in 1881. It gives the facts about an actual case of mysterious death which excited the country and occupied the newspapers, in the summer when President Garfield was dying.

Two or three persons were accused of the murder of Jennie Cramer, but they were cleared, and the girl's death is generally believed to have been the result of accident or suicide.

This real mystery furnished the starting point — little else — for the first number of a famous series of dime novels. Moreover, it introduced one of the most celebrated detectives in paper-covered fiction: Old Cap Collier, whose name was resurrected from oblivion, a few years ago, by Mr. Irvin S. Cobb.

Old Cap Collier was at first the name of the detective-hero of the series. Later his name was given to a long series of novels, still appearing in 1898, and numbering more than seven hundred titles. These were written by various authors and described the adventures of every kind of detective in all kinds of places. Some of them added to their interest by starting with a small percentage of fact.

Thus, there was "Old Cap Collier; or, 'Piping' the New Haven Mystery" (1883); "Lightning Grip, the Cautious Detective; or 'Piping' the Nathan Murder Mystery"; (in which the real Nathan case is so disguised that its best friend wouldn't know it) and "Old Cap Collier & Co.; or, 'Piping' the Stewart Vault Mystery," by Ironclad. A few weeks later, and in order to emulate his hero's fondness for a quick change into a fresh disguise, there appeared "Young Ironclad, the Keen Detective." By Old Cap Collier.

Thus, in the favorite mystifying fashion, the name of the hero is also used as a pseudonym of his creator, and later as the name of the series which he led off. The genius of the great detective broods over the scene, and his name, like sudden flashes of lightning, strikes here and there, to the utter befoozlement of the bibliographer and the historian.

The name of the author of the first of the series, and of many which followed, is given as W. I. James, and it also seems to be clouded in mystery. It probably covers the identity of a group of writers. I believe that it appears on none of his title pages. Pseudonyms were chiefly in favor with N. L. Munro, the publisher.

At first, the Old Cap Collier stories were quite unlike the other dime novels in appearance. Large pamphlets (about six by ten inches) they were without illustrations, and had rather sober, green-paper covers, which later alternated with pink and brick red. The design on each

LARGEST CIRCULATION OF ANY FIVE-CENT LIBRARY PUBLISHED.

Old Cap. Collier LIBRARY.

No. 671.

MUNRO'S PUBLISHING HOUSE,
24 & 26 Vandewater Street, New York.—October 17, 1896.

5 Cents.

OLD CAP. COLLIER LIBRARY IS ISSUED WEEKLY.—BY SUBSCRIPTION $2.00 PER ANNUM.
Entered according to act of Congress, in the year 1896, by NORMAN L. MUNRO, in the office of the Librarian of Congress, at Washington, D. C.—[Entered at Post Office, N. Y., as Second Class Matter.]

THE CROOKS AND LABYRINTHS OF NEW-YORK

or

GIDEON GAULT TRAILING A BANKER'S ASSASSINS

By Lieut. Carlton

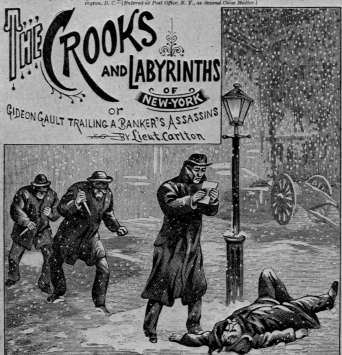

Two burly-looking men, with daggers in hand, were stealing up behind Gault.

cover, which introduced a few small pictures, was curiously staid and almost mincing. Inside, however, the purchaser easily found the worth of his money. In about eighty pages, set in two columns of murderously fine print, Old Cap dashed from adventure to adventure.

According to my compilation, in the story of the New Haven mystery, Old Cap Collier —

Gets into a fight (plain)	5 times
Fights four or five men at once	7 times
Is shot at or attacked with knives or bludgeons	12 times
Is blown up	Once
Escapes poisoning	Once
Is buried alive	Once
Is caught in a steel trap disguised as a chair	Once
Number of men he beats "to a jelly"	2
Number of men he hurls through the air [1]	21
Number of men he would have hurled through the air, but refrained, for fear of making a noise, and instead choked him until he was black in the face	1

During the same story, he assumes many disguises,

[1] One of these, a very large man, he hurled thirty feet.

putting on some of these elaborate costumes in the street, and almost in the presence of dangerous villains. An incomplete list of these disguises includes these:

1. As a fat Dutchman.
2. As an elderly man with gray hair.
3. As a countryman; very elaborate.
4. As a tramp.
5. As a sandwich-man.
6. A cabman.
7. A cavalier at a masked ball.
8. An oysterman.
9. The oysterman reversed — that is, the clothes turned inside out, with the addition of black whiskers and a wig. This was done at great speed and in a time of special stress. The author does not give a name to the character assumed; perhaps the disguise was that of a fisher for scallops.
10. As "the man he saw in the woods."
11. Elderly broker or "merchant."
12. A "country merchant."
13. A middle-aged peddler.
14. An organ grinder.
15. A ship captain. Old Cap Collier seems to have

liked the ship captain, for he wore the costume for two or three hours without change.

16. A "rough."

17. The "one he wore in the den of thieves," and

18. Another quick change, in which, apparently, he was disguised as nothing in particular, or merely a human being, for the author does not describe what it represented.

Here is the beginning of " 'Piping' the New Haven Mystery":

"Acht, neun, zehn — weg sie gehen!"

These words — which translated into English are "eight, nine, ten — away you go!" were uttered by a fat Dutchman in one of the public gardens of New Haven.

The fat Dutchman had been sitting on a bench, tranquilly smoking an immense meerschaum with a long stem, and reading a newspaper.

As he was thus engaged two men approached, and one of them said to the other:

"Here is where we are to meet the girls. It is a secluded spot; but in order that our conversation with them may be strictly private, we must get rid of that fat Dutchman."

"How is that to be done?"

"I'll show you."

The speaker walked to the Dutchman and said:

"Hans, your room's better than your company."

The Dutchman not replying, apparently not understanding the English language, the two men went a step closer, the rougher-looking of the two saying to the other:

"We'll have to punch old sauerkraut's head."

No sooner had the remark been made than the fat Dutchman arose and seized the two men by their coat collars, one with either hand.

They were both powerful men, but with a strength that was wonderful, the Dutchman pulled them close together in spite of their struggles, held them at arm's length and commenced beating their heads together.

This he did seven times, and then, as he gave them three more raps, each causing them to see stars, he uttered the words which appeared at the head of this chapter:

"Acht, neun, zehn — weg sie gehen."

As he said "away you go," the fat Dutchman exhibited strength that was simply marvelous.

He raised the two men bodily, one with each hand, and whirling them around his head, hurled them a distance of several feet.

The Dutchman folded his arms and recommenced smoking his pipe.

The two men got up, joined each other at the distance of thirty yards, and commenced rubbing their heads.

The fat Dutchman smiled, took his pipe from his mouth, yawned and stared toward them.

"Git!" said the rougher of the two men.

They took to their heels and ran.

No sooner had they disappeared than the face of the fat Dutchman relapsed into a broad smile, and as he again took his seat on the bench he said, in remarkably good English:

"I think I surprised those fellows."

Hardly had these words been uttered when two young women approached and sat down on the bench directly in front of the Dutchman.

They looked around anxiously and one of them said:

"Bruce and Hayward are behind time."

"They'll soon be along."

"How about the New Haven Mystery?"

"Oh, that's all right. But ain't it kicking up a dickens of an excitement in the country?"

"How easily we could make it plain if we wanted to."

"Hush!" said the other young woman.

"What's the matter?"

"Don't you see that man?"

"Oh, he's only a Dutchman, and the stupidest one I ever saw. I'll bet he can't speak English."

"We'll see. I say, sir!"

The fat Dutchman looked up from his paper, stared boldly at her for a moment and contented himself with a yawn.

"What did I tell you, Kate? That stupid Dutchman has just come over."

"Oh, bother the Dutchman!"

"What fools detectives are. They'll drop the case."

"Ain't it queer the detectives never struck our trail, or that of Bruce and Hayward?"

"Pshaw! detectives are fools."

At this period of the conversation an urchin approached and handed the girl called Kate a letter.

"Lord, Susan!" said she. "It's from Bruce. I know his writing."

"Oh!" said the fat Dutchman to himself. "So we have Kate and Susan. Good!"

He smoked on placidly.

The girl called Kate opened the letter, and said:

"It is from Bruce, I declare. I wonder why he wrote instead of coming."

"Why don't you read it and see, you fool?"

"It's short. 'Have been to the place and got run off. Daren't come back. There's danger in the air. Meet me to-night at nine, on the corner of Chapel and —— streets, Beware of the fat Dutchman."

"The fat Dutchman?"

The urchin interposed by saying:

"Any answer?"

"Tell him 'all right.'"

The urchin darted off. The woman, Kate, advanced to the fat Dutchman and said:

"Look here, mister, are you a spy?"

The Dutchman took his pipe out of his mouth, gazed stolidly at the speaker, and then spoke, in a phlegmatic manner, several words in German.

The woman interrupted him by exclaiming angrily:
"Can't you talk English, you stupid old mummy?"

The Dutchman looked bewildered and said helplessly:
"Yaw."

The girl, Susan, shook her fist in the face of the Dutchman, and hissed:

"You old jelly mass, if we find you're fooling us we'll kill you."

"Yaw," said the Dutchman, replacing his pipe in his mouth.

Having done which, he waddled away, seemingly afraid of the irate beauties, who were left in doubt as to his real character.

The fat Dutchman walked on until he reached a thickly-inhabited part of the city, where he entered a house and disappeared.

Presently a man came out of the house.

He must have been the Dutchman, for he said to himself.

"From what I heard those two young women, Kate and Susan, say in the garden, I think I am on the track."

But the appearance of the Dutchman was entirely changed.

He was now an elderly man with gray hair, and walked with a stick.

He also moved slowly as if the infirmities incident to old age had overtaken him.

He walked along until he reached the office of the chief of police.

[147]

It is proper to state, also, that his figure no longer presented the appearance of corpulence, but was quite slender.

"Well," he said to the chief of police, who was alone, "you sent for me, and I've come."

"I didn't send for you, my friend."

"Are you sure?"

"Yes."

"I say you did send for me."

"Look here, my contradictory old buck, if you came here to raise a row, you'll get fired out in a hurry."

The chief of police reached out his hand toward the bell, but was interrupted by the remark:

"Hold on. Didn't you send for Old Cap Collier?"

"Yes, I did. What's that got to do with you?"

"Well, *I* am Old Cap Collier."

This irritates the chief of police, who suggests that the man before him is too "weak and infirm to be able to cope with a lot of rascals."

Collier satisfied his mind on that point. Incidentally, he did to the chief what many of us must have longed to do with such high officials.

He reached down, caught the chief of police by the waistband with one hand, raised him bodily and swung him around his head with as much ease as ordinary men would have handled an infant. Then he gave him a fling, and landed him easily, and without harm, on a sofa at the other side of the room.

I like "without harm." It shows Collier's respect for the law.

The chief of police, "forgetting his dignity," remarks: "Thunder!" And Old Cap Collier suggests that they get to business, and discuss the reason for calling the detective from New York.

Says the chief:

"It's about the New Haven mystery."

"What about it?"

"We want it worked up."

"I thought it was worked up."

"Well it is not."

"The trial is ended and the accused are acquitted."

"But nothing has been proved to a certainty except that the girl was found dead. A woman of bad morals introduced herself to the girl, and it is thought, inculcated dangerous doctrines against morality into her mind."

"Did the girl know her real character?"

"No, for she was introduced as a respectable friend of two young men."

"And the result was —— "

"That the girl was ruined. Soon afterwards, her body was found on the beach."

The detective, who already knew this, said:

"It is certain, then, that she was betrayed and murdered."

"It is not sure that she was murdered."

"Why not, when she was found dead?"

"There is a theory advanced, and believed by some, that she committed suicide."

"What reasons do they give in support of that theory?"

"They believe that she was drugged, and ruined. And that when she came to herself her shame was so great that, preferring death to dishonor, she resolved to take her life, and procured arsenic for that purpose. That she wandered to the beach and there swallowed the arsenic that was found in her stomach at the *postmortem*."

"What is the other theory?"

"That, after accomplishing her ruin, the betrayers became frightened at the possible consequences of their acts, as she threatened to expose them, and appeal to the law. And that they killed her to avoid exposure."

"Assisted by the woman?"

"That is one theory. Another is that they alone, or possibly only one of them, committed the crime. Still another theory is that the woman, alarmed at the consequence of her act in lending herself to the two young men to accomplish the ruin of the girl, gave her the poison alone. But there is still another theory which although it does not seem probable, may be the correct one."

"What is it?"

"It has been hinted in anonymous letters that the murder was not committed by either of the accused parties."

"Ah!"

"But that it was done by her former lover who meant honorable marriage, and learning that she had been betrayed, become crazed with grief and rage, and, in the madness of the moment, slew the girl."

"Who was the lover?"

"We have never been able to discover."

"H'm," said Collier, "The case is rather mixed. What do you want me to do?"

"I want you to dive into this infernal mystery which has baffled the vigilance of the New Haven police. I want you to find the murderers of that poor girl."

"Then you don't believe in the theory of suicide?"

"No."

"Well, sir, I will 'pipe' this New Haven mystery until I find out who killed the girl, and bring the murderers to justice."

"Do so, and your reward shall be enormous."

Now the author tells us a little about his hero:

The detective was, in many respects, one of the most remarkable men of the present age.

To the police authorities of New York, he was known as Old Cap Collier.

He was by them, and is still, considered the most successful of detectives.

But around this remarkable man there was, even to the police authorities of New York, a veil of mystery which was simply impenetrable.

Not one of them knew what he had been before he had entered the service.

None knew whence he came, or whither he went.

His residence was a secret none could discover.

A letter sent to a certain place was sure to reach him, but he never came for it in person, neither could any one succeed in following the messenger.

His career was involved in mystery, even to those who, knowing from his works that he was the ablest of detectives, employed him to ferret out crimes which were impenetrable to other men.

Upon one fact all were agreed.

This fact was his enormous strength.

On one occasion a bully of enormous strength, weighing two hundred and fifty pounds, attacked him in the street, without cause.

Collier took him by the collar and waistband, lifted him apparently without exertion, and flung him ten feet high into the air over a loaded truck, where he fell with a broken shoulder.

It was said that Collier did not know his own strength, which was simply prodigious.

This man, who, had he been inclined to evil, and quarrelsome, would have been a terror to all people, was one of the most peaceful men living.

His nature was kind and true, and noble.

It was only to evil doers that he was terrible.

Not even to those who employed him did he disclose the means he made use of to solve mysteries which, to others, would have been impenetrable.

To the good he was a mysterious guardian; to the evil he was mysterious and terrible.

And this was the man whom the chief of police had selected to solve the mystery of the manner in which the betrayed and murdered girl came to her death.

He begins by imposing upon the crooks in this cruel fashion:

About an hour after Collier left the office of the chief of police, a lank countryman, the greenest-looking specimen imaginable, sauntered along one of the principal business streets of New Haven.

The countryman, who looked sixty-five years old, wore an old slouch hat, and coat and breeches which were several inches too short for him.

His cowhide boots were white with the dust of the road.

He wore a calico necktie, and a stand-up collar which reached to his ears.

He was smoking a corncob pipe, the stem of which was not more than two inches long.

A peculiar feature about the countryman was that instead of keeping his wallet in his pocket he gripped it tightly in his left hand.

The wallet was "fat" enough to be well filled with money, and attracted the notice of several people, including a man who looked at it searchingly, and at the countryman earnestly, and then slunk away.

It was noticed that the countryman did not go far from a particular spot, but often turned and sauntered to and fro past it.

Suddenly a man came out of a house, and tapping the countryman familiarly on the shoulder said:

"Halloo, uncle!"

"I guess yer mistaken, mister," replied the countryman, in a squeaky voice.

"Guess not. Where's the folks?"

"The folks is to hum, I reckon, mister."

"Look here, uncle, you don't seem to know me."

"I calkerlate yer have got the advantage of me a *leetle*."

"Don't you remember I was at your town a year ago?"

"Waal, no, I can't say I do, stranger."

"Well, I was."

"I want ter know! What mout yer name be, stranger?"

"John Smith."

"Psho! Yer don't say. Waal, neow, I swan by gosh, I do believe I've hearn of you before."

"Of course you have."

"I have, by gravy! Say, now, Mr. Smith, how's all yer folks ter hum?"

"Oh, they're all right. How's yours?"

"Middlin'."

"I say, uncle, what's that you've got in your hand?"

The countryman drew closer and whispered:

"Waal, neow, yer see I sold the ten-acre pastur lot fur a thousin' dollars."

"And you've got the money with you, in that wallet, I'll bet drinks."

"You're good at guessin', mister."

"What are you going to do with it?"

"I thought I'd put it in a bank."

"Right, uncle. If you'll come with me, I'll show you the best bank in the city."

"Will yer, neow? I say, mister, yer the most uncommon 'commodatin' man I've run ag'in."

"Oh, that's all right, uncle. I'll do anything for my friends. Come along."

They walked a few steps and the city man said:

"Let's take a drink."

"It's sunthin I don't often do."

"You're a teetotaler, eh?"

"Not ezackly; an' as Betsy ain't around —— "

They walked into a small, dark place, and Mr. John Smith said to the countryman:

"What'll you have, uncle?"

"I swan, I dunno. What's yourn?"

"A whiskey cocktail. That's bang up."

"Gimme a leetle o' the same, Mister Man."

Mr. Smith winked at the bar-tender, who was an ugly-looking fellow, and leaning over the counter, whispered:

"Fix his."

The bar-tender mixed the two cocktails, and added a few drops out of a small bottle, into the mixture intended for the countryman.

"Half a dollar," he said.

Mr. Smith flung the money on the counter.

"Git aout!" shouted the countryman.

He kicked at a dog that was sniffing at his heels, and missed him.

"The pesky critter's mad!" shouted the countryman, as the dog ran yelping toward the door, with his tail between his legs.

This drew the attention of Mr. John Smith and the bar-tender toward the door, and the countryman seized the opportunity to pour the contents of his glass upon the floor.

When the two men turned around, the dog having disappeared, the countryman stood with his head thrown back, and the glass inverted at his lips. Smacking his lips, he said:

"That's hunky."

Shortly afterwards, Collier provokes all the assembled ruffians into a fight, in which he hurls them right and left. Their schemes — whatever they may be — are for the moment thwarted.

He makes his escape, and appears disguised as a tramp, following a man from this den of thieves to a house in which he arrives in time to save a girl from being beaten by a strange man. The man is not strange to Collier, however, who promptly names him as Alton Spigot, and says that he has been concerned in the murder.

The names of a number of characters in the story, by the way, are singular, and indicate a determination on the part of the author to give the citizens of New Haven no cause for libel suits.

The girl who has been saved tells Old Cap Collier that the murdered girl has not really been murdered — an interesting and important point.

Collier assumes another disguise and proceeds to the house of Jule Sago, where he meets a young woman "whose face was pretty but showed marks of dissipation."

By threatening her he gets the hint to go to the burial place of the murdered girl, and search the grass at the head of the grave. He does this, and finds a bit of tin, with the advice scratched on it: "Search the vault."

He joins the first girl at an apartment on Chapel Street, and in a fresh disguise hears of her plan to go to a masked ball with the two men whom he had fought in the garden. He decides to follow them — nobody could say exactly why, except that his instinct tells him that they are all villains, and that it is safe to "shadow" them.

He hurries to the street and bribes a cabman to let him drive the carriage. His subsequent adventures are these:

"Change coats with me," said Collier, "and hats too."

The change being effected, the detective mounted the seat and drove to the corner, where he left Bruce and Kate.

Drawing up to the sidewalk, he descended from the box and throwing open the door of the coach, said:

"Now, then, lady an' gent, if ye please."

Bruce and Kate entered the carriage.

"Where to, sir?" asked Collier.

"To the masked ball."

Collier who had received instructions from the driver how to get to the masked ball, drove there.

Bruce paid his fee, and was going into the house with Kate on his arm, when the detective said to a servant who was lounging on the step:

"I shall return in an hour. If you can find out what costume that lady and gentleman assume, I will give you five dollars. Meet me here."

Without waiting for a reply, he climbed upon the seat and drove back to the driver, who said:

"Well, this is a lark."

"You're right it is. We'll change coats and hats. That's right. Here's your double X and fare. Good-night."

"Good-night," said the driver. "Well, you're a brick."

Not being in a hurry at this juncture, Collier sauntered to a costumer's and procured the dress of a cavalier, with sword, plumed hat, mask, etc.

He also donned a dark moustache, curled and twisted at the ends, *à la* Louis Napoleon.

Donning these, he put on a summer overcoat of light texture, effectually concealing his picturesque costume, as it reached nearly to his feet.

Thus accoutred, Collier returned to the house where the masked ball was in progress.

The waiter, whom he had bribed, was at the door.

"Well," said Collier, "what luck?"

"Excellent, sir."

He gave a description of the costume the woman Kate had adopted after entering the house, and added:

"You cannot mistake her. She is the only woman who has a bouquet of white roses in the bosom of her dress."

Collier paid the man his five dollars and went in, having first pulled down his mask.

The detective sauntered unnoticed among the guests, but saw nothing of the mask with the white roses in the bosom of her dress.

Becoming out of patience, at last, he said:

"The waiter must have made a mistake, and I'm bluffed."

Hardly had he said this when a mask with white roses appeared so suddenly as to leave him in doubt as to the direction whence she came.

"At last," said the detective.

It was then eleven o'clock.

She was immediately joined by a man, who, by his figure, Collier recognized as Bruce.

Sauntering to a position near them, the detective heard the man say:

"I tell you, Katie, you must go."

"But I'm afraid."

"Of what?"

"Of the shadows of that awful place."

"Bah! Who's afraid of shadows?"

"Why don't you go?"

"I've other business."

"But not so fearful as this."

"I don't see what there is fearful in it."

"The time, the place."

"I tell you, Kate, it must be done. The time was never so propitious. That done, we can defy the sleuth-hounds who are moving Heaven and earth to clear up the New Haven mystery."

"Well, I'll go. The ghosts can but kill me."

"Then I'll be off to the other business."

Bruce moved away.

Collier stepped closer, and said, in a rough voice:

"Come, let's dance."

Kate turned indignantly, and replied:

"Sir, you insult me."

"Not half so much as you insulted the fat Dutchman this morning. The cops are on your track, my chicken. You'd better git."

Frank Starr's TEN CENT

American ★ Novels

Number 145.

OLD RUBE, THE HUNTER.

FRANK STARR & CO., 41 PLATT STREET, N. Y.

The American News Company, New York

(See page 262)

Collier assumed this rôle of insult with a purpose.

He was afraid Kate would weaken, and not go on the terrible errand Bruce had proposed.

If the errand were successfully accomplished, Bruce had said, she would be safe. And, if she were assured that the police were on her track, she would hasten on the errand, no matter how fearful it was, to secure her safety, before they caught her.

His words had the desired effect.

Kate turned pale beneath her mask, hastened to the dressing-room and changed her costume for a street dress, and left the house.

Hastily donning his long overcoat, and exchanging his plumed hat for a slouched one he took from the pocket of the coat, Collier followed.

The woman walked rapidly.

Before long the detective saw that she was going in the direction of the cemetery.

She entered the cemetery, and threading her way among the graves, stopped before the door of a vault.

The detective thought of the words on the piece of tin:

"Search the vault."

Collier believed that he was on the point of unearthing a mystery.

This woman was searching the vault.

What was it she expected to find there?

At this instant, his eyes being riveted on the woman, through the crack of the door, Collier received a tremendous push from behind.

Giant in strength as he was, he could not resist this push, being balanced, as it were, on a pivot.

He lost his balance and fell forward, pushing the door open and falling inside the vault.

At the same time the door was pulled to and locked on the outside.

Collier sprang to his feet, tried the door and found it locked.

"Hum!" he said.

Turning to the woman, he saw that she was standing gasping, her arm resting on a casket, as though to steady herself. Her eyes were staring at him, and her face was ashen with fear.

The detective was about to step forward when a voice, the owner of which could not be seen, hissed:

"Fool, put out that light."

Instantly the woman seemed to recover courage. She moved the slide of the lantern, hiding the light.

The place was dark as a dungeon.

The detective could hear Kate's labored breathing, and also thought he distinguished a slight sound on his left.

There were, then, three living occupants of the vault.

Collier and the girl, Kate, were two. Who was the third?

The detective listened.

In a moment no noise was heard.

Then the silence was broken by the slight, clicking sound, which follows the cocking of a pistol, when the person who does it is not expert enough to pull back gently on the trigger at the same instant he raises the hammer.

"Oho!" said Collier to himself. "Is that it? Well, then, my murderously-inclined companion, two sometimes play at that game."

And the detective, noiselessly shifting his position a little, placed himself on the defensive.

The detective felt himself thoroughly able to cope with the third party in the vault.

The woman Kate, he made no account of at the present juncture, because she was already half frightened to death.

She could give a man as good as he sent when she stood in no danger of physical harm.

But when it came to a time of danger she weakened, and became confused.

The third party in the vault was a man.

This was certain, because when he said to Kate: "Fool, put out the light!" the voice was harsh and masculine.

Collier determined to first get the better of the man, and then have it out with the girl, Kate.

Among the many accomplishments of the detective, was the power of throwing his voice from one point to another.

He threw his voice about five feet to the left and said: "St!"

The sound was instantly followed by the report of a pistol in the hands of the third party.

The flash revealing plainly the place where the man stood, Collier sprang forward, and was [so] fortunate as to catch hold of his arm.

A single wrench of the detective's giant strength caused the man to cry out with pain, and drop the pistol.

Collier then raised the man, and hurled him down on the floor of the vault.

Then, assuming the voice of the man, the detective said, in a low voice:

"Kate!"

"Is it you, Hicks!"

"Yes."

"I did not expect to see you in the vault."

"You have not seen me yet."

"Did you enter after I did?"

"Not much."

"I didn't see you."

"I was hid behind the coffins."

"What were you doing here?"

"I wanted to see the inside of the vault."

"Bah! You've seen dozens, you body-snatcher. Don't try to fool me."

"H'm!" said the detective to himself, "how she's giving it to me. Well, I'm finding out the character of Hicks, at any rate."

"Come," repeated Kate, in a shrill voice, "what were you doing here?"

"I'll tell you, if you'll tell me."

"Tell you what?"

"What *you* were doing here."

"That is none of your business."

"Then what I was doing here is none of *your* business."

"Is that all you've got to say?"

"It is, my chicken."

"Then, get out of here."

Collier heard the click of the lock of a small revolver, as the hammer was raised.

Thinking himself unable to dodge a bullet at such close quarters, Collier said:

"Hold on, Kate."

"Will you get out!"

"Yes, but I would rather make friends and tell you what I came here for."

"Well, then, do it."

"Strike a light first."

Kate opened the slide of the dark lantern. The vault was flooded with light.

At the instant her figure was disclosed, Collier snatched at the pistol and obtained it.

"Euchered!" he said.

Kate, when she saw it was not Hicks, sprang back until brought to a stop by the nearest casket, and said:

"What do you want here?"

"A little business with you."

"I'll have nothing to do with you. Look here, ain't you the man that insulted me at the ball?"

"Oh, no."

"I say 'yes' you hound," shrieked Kate, beside herself with rage.

"Don't 'get on your ear,' my daisy," said Collier, adopting the slang language of Kate.

"I want you to leave the vault."

"Well, now, I must say your request's reasonable."

"Why don't you comply, then?"

"I'll tell you why. I don't believe either of us will get out in a hurry because the door of the vault is locked on the outside."

"Heaven!"

"They've got us all in here."

"Who?"

"I don't know; but I guess they mean to keep us."

"We'll suffocate."

"I suppose so. Hadn't we better come to terms?"

"What do you propose?"

"That you tell me why you came here."

"I refuse."

"Well, then, you won't get anything out of me."

"If you won't go, I will."

"I'm willing, but the door's locked."

Looking toward the door, Collier saw to his astonishment that it stood open.

It must have been opened noiselessly by someone on the outside.

What was the reason of this singular proceeding?

Why should the door first have been locked and then thrown wide open?

Kate had not been accompanied to the vault by any person.

Was, then, the mysterious person on the outside a confederate of Hicks?

Having possession of the pistol of Kate, and the man on the floor, Collier no longer felt fear of the persons in the vault.

Turning to Kate he said harshly:

"Stand still."

"I will not."

The detective being on his mettle, said in a very harsh tone:

"If you don't, I'll treat you roughly."

"Beast!" said Kate.

"That's all right. But don't you stir."

"Where are you going?"

"Outside."

"All right. I suppose I can stay here."

"Don't you attempt to escape."

Having said this, Collier went outside the vault and looked around.

The cemetery appeared vacant.

There might have been someone behind the tombstones, but he thought it too risky to investigate, and, returning, was near the door of the vault when a voice said, sounding on the right:

"I say!"

The detective turned around.

A shadow on the right appeared to be sneaking off at a slow pace.

"Hold on," said Collier.

"Go to the devil," said the voice.

Irritated beyond his customary coolness, Collier, against his better judgment, leveled his pistol and fired at the shadow.

"Ha! ha!" laughed the voice.

The detective sprang forward.

He reached the tombstone where he had last seen the shadow.

Nothing was there except the white marble of which the headstone was composed, and the green grass that, growing rank, covered the grave.

Collier, mystified, stopped and listened. Silence reigned in the graveyard.

Collier searched around. No one could be seen.

"Strange," said the detective.

He stood a moment, and then a sudden thought occurred to him.

He ran back to the vault. The woman, Kate, was just coming out.

He caught her and pushed her back, and in his excitement, the detective had exerted too much of his giant strength.

The girl commenced crying.

This was the surest way to disarm the giant detective.

A dozen men could not make him "take water" half as quickly as the tears of one woman.

"You hurt me," she said.

The detective was about to reply, when he noticed that the man Hicks was gone.

"Halloo!" he said.

"What's the matter?"

"Hicks is missing."

"Is he?"

"Yes, you know that very well. Where is he gone?" said Collier.

"He got up and went out two minutes ago."

"Which way?"

"How do I know when I couldn't see out of the door of the vault?"

The detective felt strongly inclined to shake the girl. He resisted because she was a woman.

Releasing her, he said:

"You know very well that I have you in my power. Tell me about the murdered girl."

"What do you want to know?"

"Is she dead?"

"Certainly. I was at her funeral."

"Who killed her?"

"How do I know?"

"Pshaw!" said Collier. "Everybody knows who was accused of it."

"What everybody says must be true."

"That is always the case."

The detective considered a moment and then said:

"Do you know the young men who were tried for the murder and acquitted?"

"Goodness, no!"

"Don't lie, Kate. I know better."

"*How* do you know better?"

"From information I've received."

Kate at that instant started and said:

"You're the Dutchman Susan and I saw in the public garden this morning."

"The Dutchman!"

"Don't try to make strange of it. I thought I had seen you before, and now I am certain."

The detective finding himself discovered, tried no longer to keep up the deception, but said in the coolest voice imaginable:

"I believe you know more about the death of the girl than you care to confess."

The girl, with an insolent laugh made a movement, and had turned out of the vault, the detective's back being toward the door, when there came the report of a pistol from that quarter.

A bullet whistled past Collier's head and buried itself in one of the coffins.

Kate uttered a cry.

Collier sprang toward the door. He looked out but could see no one.

He ran entirely around the vault. No person was in sight. He stopped and in spite of his strong nerve, shivered. First he had chased a shadow which had vanished in the graveyard.

And second he had been fired at by a person whom he could not see.

Was the person the man Hicks, who had been overcome by the detective in the vault?

No, he had disarmed Hicks.

BEADLE'S POCKET Library

Copyrighted, 1884, by Beadle and Adams. Entered at the Post Office at New York, N. Y., as Second Class Mail Matter. May 28, 1884.

Vol. II. $2.50 a Year.   Published Weekly by Beadle and Adams, No. 98 William St., New York.   Price, Five Cents.   No. 20.

ROARING RALPH ROCKWOOD, The Reckless Ranger.

By Harry St. George.

CHAPTER I.

THE PRAIRIE PESTS.

THE sharp, whip-like crack of a rifle awoke a thousand echoes among the distant foot-hills, and broke the stilly silence of the night. Following the shot came the shrill neigh of a horse and then once more stillness.

A person with remarkably keen ears might have caught the low but hearty curse, that

(See page 263)

Who then was it?

By the exercise of a little of his common sense, Collier disabused himself of the idea that it was a spirit or anything else supernatural.

Ghosts do not fire powder and ball.

It was then someone who had mysteriously disappeared and left no trace behind.

Realizing the danger of exposing himself to a second shot of the enemy, Collier saw the necessity of again getting under cover.

He was not afraid of a dozen ordinary men in a street fight, barring pistols, but he could not dodge, neither could he defend himself against a pistol bullet.

Shortly afterwards, Collier gets himself arrested in company with two of the villains. He is again told that the murdered girl has been seen alive. Finally, he himself sees her in a gambling-house.

It appears that the morals of the heroes of dime novels had suffered a grievous change from the old days.

Formerly they were not only teetotallers, but anti-tobacconists. Collier, however, not only smokes but drinks with the worst of them, and in this scene engages in a game which I take to be poker. None of these vices impairs his splendid physical strength, however, and he is perpetually chivalrous to women.

The gambling house is frequented by an unpleasant

person, a prize-fighter, with a weakness for gouging out the eyes of his adversaries. His name is Strunket Brax. Here is the end of the game. Collier is disguised as a "country merchant" or something of that order.

"Bet yer another hundred ye hain't."

"I thought all your money was on the board."

"Mebbe I cud manage to scrape another hundred out uv my old clothes."

"All right, old gentleman. Plank your tin."

The money was deposited on the table.

"Show up," said Collier.

The prize-fighter turned his cards face upward, and said:

"Here they are, four aces."

"I don't see 'em. There's three aces, a queen and a six." As quick as a flash, Collier swept the money from the table and put it in his pocket.

"Hold on!" shouted the prize-fighter. "I had four aces."

"Guess not, mister."

"I'll swear I had."

"Where are they?"

This question "stumped" the prize-fighter, who shouted:

"You infernal old cheat!"

"Look here, mister, be a leetle keerful."

"Give me that money or I'll punch your head."

[172]

"You don't draw water enough."

"H — l and fury!" roared the prize-fighter. "Let me get at him."

He rushed at Collier. The gamblers stood off, not attempting to interfere.

They were sure that in about ten seconds the detective would be pounded to a jelly and his money abstracted from his pockets and divided among them.

Then he would be kicked ignominiously into the street.

The reader can imagine their astonishment when, in less than a minute the bully was knocked out of time.

The gamblers began to perceive that they had caught a Tartar, and instead of "taking in" they had been "taken in."

Determined not to miss the money, with one impulse they sprang upon the apparent old man.

Collier was now in his glory.

To punish rascals was his pastime.

His wonderful strength was now exerted to its utmost.

Catching up one of the gamblers he hurled him against the other with the force of a battering ram.

The next man he whirled around his head and hurled out of the window.

The others followed until the room remained clear of all except Collier and the prize-fighter, who walked toward the door.

"You can't go out that way."

"Which way, then?"

"Through the window. Follow your fellow rascals."

The prize-fighter climbed through the window and disappeared.

Collier now remained alone in the room.

He laughed and said:

"I have taught these fellows a pretty lesson about 'plucking a pigeon'."

And he continued:

"I must find that girl."

He searched the house from top to bottom.

"H'm," he said, "I expected as much. She's gone."

He returned to the lower hall and saw, confronting him, the negro.

"Look here, Sambo," he said, "who was the girl that entered this house half an hour ago?"

"Didn't none come in."

Realizing that it would be impossible to extract any information from the negro, Collier said:

"Stand aside and let me out."

"I ain't goin' for to let you out."

"Oh, you're going to keep me prisoner, eh?"

"Dat's it," said the negro.

Collier smiled and asked:

"Well, Sambo, would you like to have me break your neck?"

"You can't do it, white man."

Collier strode forward, parried a terrible blow, and catching the negro by the neck, hurled him over his head to the other end of the hall. Then he said:

"Good-by Sambo; I'll see you later."

Collier returns to the vault, in company with an ally, a boy who has had the misfortune to lose his tongue. He is called "the tongueless lad." They pick the lock of the vault and the detective begins an investigation, the boy acting as guard, outside.

The boy is attacked by a stray ruffian, whom Collier promptly overcomes, handcuffs, and drags inside the vault. Frightened at the threat of being left within this place, the ruffian offers to reveal "the secret of the vault." He says:

"Open that coffin and you'll see something that'll take the starch out of you."

"Oho, I'll have the starch taken out of me, shall I?" said Collier.

"I didn't say I'd do it."

"You didn't?"

"No. I said if you open that coffin you'll see something that'll take the starch out of you."

"If you attempt to escape while I'm opening the casket, I'll catch you and lock you up in the vault."

"Don't fret; I tumble and lay still."

"Get around on the other side of me."

"What's that for?"

"I want to be between you and the door."

The man having moved to the place indicated, Collier said:

"What's your name?"

"Snifftin."

"Very good, Mr. Snifftin. Now behave yourself, or I'll do worse than lock you up in the vault."

Collier, who had brought a screw-driver along, unscrewed the lid of the casket.

Raising the lid, he saw a beautiful face, in a perfect state of preservation.

The face was that of a young girl.

The eyes were closed. The face was slightly flushed. She looked as if she were sleeping.

Her little hands were crossed upon her bosom.

Her expression was calm and peaceful.

"Well, are you astonished?" said Snifftin.

"Yes."

"What's the matter, then."

"It's because the girl is the very image of —— "

"Well, go ahead."

"The girl who was found at Savin Rock."

"It's the same girl."

This was a lie and Collier knew it. The betrayed and murdered girl had been dead for months.

It was impossible for a body that had been dead so long to preserve the appearance of this one, unless it had been embalmed, which had not been the case with the murdered girl.

The girl whose form reposed in the casket had not been dead a week.

But it was fully as evident that Snifftin wished the detective to *believe* this girl was the one who was murdered at Savin Rock.

The detective humoring him, said:

"I see, my friend, that you're right; but it's generally supposed that the girl is buried outside."

"That's so."

"How, then, came she here?"

"That's more than I can say."

"Well, you'll have to confess."

"Well, suppose I won't."

"Then I'll lock you up."

"Well, then, to save myself, I'll tell you the rest of the mystery of this vault."

"Proceed."

"Do you see that coffin on the right?"

"I do."

"Open it, and you'll find out."

Collier unscrewed the lid of the second casket.

He raised the lid, and a frightful explosion followed.

The casket was blown to atoms, and Collier fell back on the floor.

For two or three minutes the detective remained not exactly insensible, but stunned and confused.

He then arose, and saw that both Dick and Snifftin were missing.

Hardly had he made this discovery when the man who attended to the cemetery, having heard the noise of the explosion, came running in and exclaimed:

"What are you doing here?"

"Looking around."

"You've been smashing things up."

"Not I. Do you know how this came about?"

"No."

"There was a torpedo in that coffin."

"You're as crazy as a March hare!"

"That's where you're wrong."

"You've no business here."

"You're wrong again."

"What's your business, then?"

"I'll ask you a question or two first."

"Hum!"

"Did you see a man and boy leave this vault after the explosion?"

"I saw a man leave the cemetery, and a boy follow on some distance behind."

"Who owns this vault?"

"Mr. Livingstone."

"Pshew!" whistled Collier.

"What's the matter?"

"Nothing; I was only thinking."

"You'll think harder when you're in the lock-up."

"Don't be in a hurry about it."

"I don't intend to be. I'm going to keep you here until Mr. Livingstone comes."

"Is he to be here to-day?"

"I'm expecting him every minute."

"Well, here he is."

Perceiving the door open, the merchant entered the vault.

Observing Collier, he said:

"Why, you're the man —— "

"Who was in your store this morning."

"What are you doing in my family vault?"

"I've business here."

"What do you want to know?"

"Who is the girl in this coffin?"

Mr. Livingstone looked, and then, with a cry of astonishment exclaimed:

"I don't know the girl."

"You never saw her before?"

"No."

"How then, came she buried in your vault?"

"It's a mystery to me."

"There's another mystery connected with this vault."

"What is it?"

"That it contains an empty coffin."

"Are you crazy."

"No, sir. The coffin that was blown to pieces by the torpedo, contained no body."

Mr. Livingstone imparts the fact that the coffin had contained the body of his deceased wife, and again expresses his annoyance at having his family vault overrun by perfect strangers. Collier makes himself known, and tells the merchant that he is investigating — "piping" is the word he uses, even in these sepulchral precincts — the New Haven mystery. Furthermore, Henry and George Harris, the men accused of the girl's murder, are innocent; but that the persons who "instigated the betrayal and murder of that girl" have designs upon the peace and honor of the Livingstones.

This they have indicated by stealing the body of the late Mrs. Livingstone; stealing Mr. Livingstone's securities; and placing an extraneous dead body within the Livingstone vault. They are going too far. It is, as Old Cap remarks, "a grand scheme of villainy."

Let us skip forty or fifty pages, and look in again at Chapter 98.

The thieves were sitting still, some playing cards and some smoking, while others drank, and all waiting for the return of Collier with the news of Brax.

When he entered the room with a rush they sprang up, crying:

"What's the matter?"

Collier cried out:

"The game's up!"

He sprang upon the rascals, and exerting his Herculean strength caught two of them by the girdle and slinging them around his head, raised them high in the air and dashed them down.

He then sprang upon another, and seizing him by the feet, swung him around, knocking down the others pell-mell.

The policemen had also taken a hand, and before the thieves hardly knew what was the matter with them, they were down upon the floor and every rascal of them handcuffed.

They sat up and looked at Collier in astonishment.

The detective laughed and said:

"Gentlemen. I hope I see you."

One of the largest of the robbers rejoined, with a string of oaths:

"Did you do this, Jack Simpson?"

"I'm the man."

The robber scowled fiercely, and said:

"I'll get even with you."

"You'd better wait until you get out of jail."

"Oh, I'll get out."

"When you're carried out on your cooling-board."

The robber scowled fiercely, and said:

"You've got nothing against me."

"I've enough against you to hang you."

"You lie."

"Do I?"

"Of course you do, for we've done nothing since you've been a member of our gang."

"That makes no difference. I've been looking for you for some time."

"Where?"

"In New York. Perhaps you remember the robbery of the Manhattan Bank."

The thief uttered a cry of alarm and exclaimed:

"Who in the name of the devil are you?"

"In the name of justice, and the detection of scoundrels, I am called Old Cap Collier."

The wretch fell back, crying:
"I am lost."

Collier proceeds to interview, at a "milk and pie shop,"
a girl named Hannah, who has been the sweetheart of
the chief rascal.

The arch-villain is named Hicks. Hannah had known
grief, but she had "toiled upward through many ob-
stacles, and remained virtuous," even amid the tempta-
tions of a milk and pie shop.

Naturally she now felt badly; but time, the great
healer, will do much to assuage grief, and the detective
knew that after awhile Hannah would find peace, and
be, thereafter, a wiser woman.

He thought it best to dwell no longer upon her blasted
love, and said:

"Hannah, you told me to come here and you would
give Hicks away."

"I'll do it."

"Is the girl who was found dead at Savin Rock the
one she was thought to be?"

"Yes."

"Are the two young men and the woman who were
tried for the murder guilty?"

"No."

"Who, then?"

"Hicks."

"Did he have assistance?"

"No."

"He, then, alone is guilty of the crime?"

"He is."

"How do you know?"

"He told me so, in a burst of confidence, when drunk."

And Hannah continued:

"He never meant to kill the girl."

"He didn't?"

"No; but he meant to commit murder all the same."

The detective, mystified, said:

"I don't understand you."

Hannah continued:

"It was a case of mistaken identity."

"Enlighten me."

"I think I can make it clear to you. Hicks, for some reason, desired the death of a certain girl, and laid his plans to that effect. He wrote a note to her asking her to meet him at Savin Rock. At the time appointed he went there. No one was there.

"He waited. After awhile the girl who was murdered came. She so greatly resembled the girl whose death Hicks desired, he thought his victim was near. Had he spoken to her and had she replied he would have ascertained his mistake, and she would have been saved.

"He waited behind a rock until she came within reach. She appeared to be utterly wretched. She was weeping and wringing her hands. Something had occurred which had caused her to be unhappy.

"She had, it is supposed, come out to that solitary place to be alone with her grief.

"Hicks waited until she came within reach, as I have said, and then there being no one in sight, he sprang out from behind the rock, threw one arm around her and put his hand over her mouth to stifle her cries.

"He then dragged her to the water's edge and held her head under until she was drowned.

"Then he dropped her. Her face came up to the surface of the water, and then, and not until then, he discovered his mistake, and found that he had committed a useless murder."

The detective, more terrified than he had ever been in his life, exclaimed:

"Good God! The wretch!"

"The basest wretch that ever lived."

Hannah continued:

"Finding that he had killed the wrong girl, Hicks was horrified and alarmed; not that he was stricken with remorse for the deed, but because he did not know who the girl was, and did not know how much of a hue and cry would be raised about the tragedy."

"What did he do?"

"He dragged the body further into the water, after filling the clothing with sand, to give the appearance of the girl having been drowned by accident and washed ashore, for he knew that the tide would soon carry it high and dry upon the sand. He then left the place, not, however, waiting for the other girl, who did not come at all."

This, then, was the solution of part of the New Haven mystery; the murderer was at last found, without the shadow of doubt, but a great part of the mystery yet remained undiscovered, without which the case would not be complete.

The detective must continue until all was known.

He said:

"Who was the girl he wished to kill?"

"I have never been able to find out."

"Did he afterwards kill her?"

"I think not."

"What led him to abandon his intention?"

"I imagine that he did not dare commit two murders so near each other."

"Do you know the reason why he wished to kill the other girl?"

"I do not; but I am certain it was in pursuance of a gigantic plan he had formed."

"And you have no idea what the plot was?"

"Not the slightest."

"Well," said the detective, "I will find out before the day is over."

And it is needless to say that he does find out. The last scene and the capture of the fiend takes place in the house of a woman named Pittenger. Collier, accompanied by a group of policemen, goes thither, and, before entering, issues his instructions:

"We will, with the exception of four men, two of

whom will be stationed at the front, and two at the back of the house, enter and search for Hicks. If he attempts to escape, and succeeds in getting out of the house, the men on the outside must show him no mercy."

Having said this, and they by that time having arrived at the house, the detective disposed of his forces.

Two he left on the sidewalk in front of the house, and two he led through an alley to the rear.

He gave them all instructions to shoot Hicks before allowing him to escape; for Collier's blood was up, and he did not intend to have Hicks slip through his fingers this time.

The others he told to follow him, and going to the door rang the bell.

A woman came to the door, to whom Collier said: "Who lives here?"

"Mrs. Pittenger."

"I wish to see her."

"She doesn't receive strangers."

Collier replied harshly:

"Well, you tell her to march along here, or we'll hand her and all that is in the house over to the law."

Terrified at this rejoinder, the woman replied:

"I am Mrs. Pittenger."

"I thought so. Well, madam, you have a rascal in this house. We want him."

"There is nobody in the house but my sister and myself."

"Then you deny that Hicks is here?"

"I don't know such a man."

"We'll search the house."

"I cannot allow that."

"Madam, you cannot prevent it."

Telling the policeman to see that the woman did not escape, the detective forced his way into the house, and commenced his search.

He first descended to the cellar, and found no traces of Hicks.

He then searched the next floor with the same result.

He then went to the other floor and found nobody there but a bed-ridden old woman in the last stages of consumption.

She appeared frightened, and said to him:

"Are you a robber?"

"No, madam. I'm searching for a rascal."

"He isn't here."

Collier rejoined sternly:

"Madam, you are too near death for lies. Tell no more of them. He is behind that panel in the wall."

While Collier talked to the woman he had been glancing critically around the room. He was rewarded by seeing a portion of the wall move, as though a person was changing his position.

He instantly came to the conclusion that Hicks was concealed there, and going to the wall kicked it. A portion of the wall gave way, disclosing an aperture. And in the aperture stood Hicks.

The rascal, as soon as he saw that he was discovered, fired a pistol at Collier and missed.

He then dashed out and tried to escape by running. Collier, who was on the lookout for this dodge, caught him and, swinging him around his head, flung him against the opposite wall.

By this time the two policemen who had remained in the hall, hearing the fracas, came up.

Hicks sat up. Collier said to him:

"You see you cannot escape. And even if you succeed in leaving this room the house is surrounded on every side."

Hicks turned frightfully pale.

His teeth were clenched and his breath came hard.

Suddenly he cried out:

"I'll never swing. I'll die right here, and you shall die with me."

As quick as thought he fired his pistol at Collier, who staggered back.

Hicks then, before they could stop him, put the revolver to his forehead and fell back dead.

The woman on the bed sprang up to a sitting posture and cried out:

"Oh, my son. Dead — dead!"

The effort was too much for her. The blood gushed from her mouth and there was a gurgling sound, she fell back on the bed.

Mother and son were dead.

Collier shuddered, and said:

"Great Heavens, this is awful."

And, iron-hearted as he was, he turned sick and faint and turned away, saying to the policemen:

"See that they are attended to."

So the New Haven mystery is a mystery no longer, and the sensation of a trial of the real murderer of the poor girl who was driven to death at Savin Rock avoided.

But she sleeps in her grave avenged, and the two young men who were deemed guilty were proven to be innocent. Henceforth let the public so believe it, for it is true.

Collier had the satisfaction of unearthing the mystery after all others had failed, and in addition he obtained a substantial reward.

In conclusion, we have only to say that there will soon be a double wedding at the merchant's house.

Brax, who has entirely recovered and reformed, has an invitation and will be there, accompanied by the cigar-girl, whom he married before he left the hospital.

And Old Cap Collier has been heard to say that he intends to kiss both brides, and dance a hornpipe at the wedding.

In brains, in powers of analysis, Cap Collier would not have had a chance against Sherlock Holmes, and still less against Holmes' fat and lazy brother, Mycroft, whose intellect was as much greater as his physical energy was less than Sherlock's. But in action, in his extraordinary ability in a fight, and in his love for all the hocus-pocus of disguise — sometimes assumed for the sheer joy of "dressing up" — he had the qualities which his boy readers loved.

Mr. Irvin Cobb in his "Plea for Old Cap Collier" made a telling point of these qualities of the dime novel — or rather, as he says, of the "nickul libruries," which were what boys of his generation used to read.

The items in "Old Cap Collier Library," published by Norman L. Munro, and viewed at this late day, are rather sad-looking pamphlets. Cap Collier himself, as the hero, has almost entirely disappeared. Here is one dated July 1, 1889: "Who Murdered Dr. Cronin? or, Shadowing the Real Criminals." By Old Cap Collier. This, of course, purports to be about a real case. And here is one nearly ten years later: "The Crime of the Old Pear Tree Farm: or, Rody Rogan on the Worthington Case." By Bernard Wayde. This is Number 735, dated January 8, 1898, when they were issued weekly. The paper is the shoddiest, and the pictures the crudest, of any I have seen.

III

THE DETECTIVES: OLD SLEUTH

IN 1889 there was being argued before the Supreme Court in the County of New York the case of George Munro *vs.* Beadle and Adams — his old employers. The point at issue was the ownership of "Old Sleuth." Mr. Munro had formerly proceeded against other publishers for a similar alleged offence.

In the course of his argument, the learned counsel amused the Court with a brief description of the rise and progress of Old Sleuth, showing that he went back farther than most of us imagine. He said, in part:

"All the numbers of *The Old Sleuth Library,* which is a serial, contain fictitious stories, first published in *The Fireside Companion,* describing the feats of a detective, written by the same author, Harlan P. Halsey, under the pseudonym Old Sleuth. Halsey, although under both his own name and his *nom de plume* is, probably, unknown to the members of this Court and also to most literary critics, is undoubtedly the most popular writer in the English language. He writes, not for the four hundred who, according to Mr. Ward Mc-

Allister, are the only persons worthy of consideration in New York society; nor even for the upper ten thousand. His audience is counted by the million. His themes are such as have always interested the majority of mankind. Mild and maidenly modesty molested by vile and vicious villainy. Cunning and cowardly crime foiled and frustrated by vigorous and victorious virtue. His scenes are laid, not in English country shires, nor in Swiss boarding-houses, nor in the unexplored parts of Africa, but on the Bowery, Broadway and Staten Island. His heroes live, not in the middle ages nor in the times of the Puritans or the Jacobites, but when Fernando Wood or Grace or Hewitt was mayor. He prides himself on the moral purity of his writings; and, on that account, since the defendants' stories describe looser incidents, does his publisher feel especially aggrieved. Although his incidents and style may be too pronounced for those of us who are pleased by the modern school of fiction, they are perfectly adapted to the tastes of hundreds of thousands who read them with avidity. His most successful work, the initial number of *The Old Sleuth Library,* first published in *The Fireside Companion* in 1872, is called 'Old Sleuth, the Detective.' It describes the exploits of a young detective who assumes the disguise of an old man and performs some exploits before which

Old Sleuth Library

THE GIANT DETECTIVE'S LAST "SHADOW."
BY "OLD SLEUTH."

A SERIES OF THE MOST THRILLING DETECTIVE STORIES EVER PUBLISHED.

No. 89.

SINGLE NUMBER.

GEORGE MUNRO'S SONS, PUBLISHERS,
Nos. 17 to 27 Vandewater Street, New York.

PRICE 5 CENTS.

Vol. IV.

Old Sleuth Library, Issued Quarterly.—By Subscription, Twenty-five Cents per Annum.
Entered at the Post Office at New York as Second-class Matter.—March 19, 1898.
(Copyrighted, 1898, by George Munro's Sons.)

The Giant Detective's Last "Shadow."

A TALE OF HERCULEAN DETECTIVE ADVENTURES.

BY "OLD SLEUTH."

NEW YORK: GEORGE MUNRO'S SONS, PUBLISHERS, 17 TO 27 VANDEWATER STREET.

those of the Admirable Crichton and Baron Munchausen pale into insignificance. The popularity of the tale was so great that it was republished several times in *The Fireside Companion,* and that Halsey wrote for the same weekly other stories, with the same fictitious character as the protagonist, such as 'Old Sleuth in Harness Again,' 'Old Sleuth's Triumph' and 'Old Sleuth in Philadelphia,' all of which except the last are republished in *The Old Sleuth Library.* In each of these, the hero is the same and is called in the body of the book Old Sleuth or Sleuth indifferently. Halsey has never written under his own name, being in fact anxious to conceal from his friends the kind of literature that he manufactures. He has used a variety of pseudonyms, among others Tony Pastor (by the permission of the actor who previously assumed that name, and many of whose songs he wrote), Judson R. Taylor and Wolf O'Neill. George Munro, however, soon discovered that it was through reference to the character Sleuth that such stories became most popular; and consequently, when publishing later stories, at first described them as 'by the author of Old Sleuth the Detective,' and subsequently by the sobriquet, Old Sleuth, which was first given him by plaintiff's son, George W. Munro.

"The name Sleuth is undoubtedly suggested by the

word sleuth-hound. But Halsey was the first to use it
as the name of a detective, or in fact as a proper name
of any kind.

"His originality was as great in this respect as was that
of Samuel Warren in naming the celebrated firm of
Quirk, Gammon & Snap, which plays so prominent a
part in 'Ten Thousand a Year.' The character and the
books in which he figured gained enormous popularity;
due partly to their intrinsic merit, partly to the efforts
of the plaintiff, who spent more than $200,000 in advertis-
ing the name.

"As usual, the plaintiff's rivals sought to reap the
profits due to the fame of his publications. A swarm of
spurious Sleuth stories have flooded the market, each
published in a library similar in form and price to those
of the plaintiff and each simulating his titles as nearly
as their publishers dare. One or two of these came out
before *The Old Sleuth Library* was instituted; but all,
long after Old Sleuth had become famous through the
joint efforts of Halsey and the plaintiff. All but those
by these defendants have been enjoined."

The Old Sleuth of that remote day is certainly forgotten. The stories signed by him in the eighties and
nineties are probably still within the recollection of

somebody, and in order to recall the style, and especially the slang of the underworld, as he represented it, I will quote from the opening pages of "Old Electricity; The Lightning Detective." By Old Sleuth. It appeared in 1885.

The story opens:

"Don't wink your peepers, Larry."

"What's up, cull?"

"That's what's up. Keep your eyelids raised for strangers."

"Oh, stash it! and throw in your light, chummie. What's the 'peep' now?"

"Things are 'clouding.' Old Electricity is mousing around."

"The devil you say! Do you suppose he's 'piping' on this 'lay' in hand?"

"Yes, blast his buttons; he's worse than forked lightning. Just when you think your 'layout' is all right, he's sure to 'flash his glim' in on you."

This conversation occurred between two remarkable-looking men standing on the platform of the Vincennes station of the Ohio and Mississippi Railroad.

One of them was a tall, wiry-looking man, possessing keen eyes, a slender, hooked nose, thin lips, and a broad, square chin.

His companion, on the contrary, whom he had addressed as Larry, was a short, thick-set man, possessing a powerful frame, and rough, villainous features.

The ugly expression of the latter's countenance was enhanced by a cast in one of his eyes, and a hideous scar, which ran across his cheek clear around to his ear.

Stretched out upon a bench which ran along the side of the station, was a man whose singular individuality was not less marked and striking than the two above described.

As he lay stretched upon the bench, it was easy to perceive that he was a man tall in stature. Long, straight yellow hair swept down upon his shoulders.

His features were small and regular and gave to a man of his stature a listless and effeminate appearance.

He wore neither mustache nor whiskers. His mouth was small, and there was a smile which played around his lips that was simply "childlike and bland."

As he lay there, carelessly biting at the handle of an umbrella, his eyes, which were dark-blue, were apparently as expressionless as those of a dozing cat.

Of all those gathered upon the platform, this singular-looking man, who looked much like "ye ancient" Yankee school-master, was seemingly the most indifferent to the scenes transpiring about.

His wardrobe was in accordance with the other seeming contrarieties of his appearance.

He wore a colored shirt, surmounted by a white collar, and a snow-white cravat.

His coat was a shabby frock, with long skirts.

Some other person had evidently been originally measured for the vest that he wore, as the extreme points, where it buttoned in front, just met the band of his pants, while on either side his shirt was visible, as also the tips of his suspenders.

His pants were blue and tight-fitting, and like his waistcoat, had evidently been cut from a piece of cloth that ran short, as they descended but half-way down his boot-tops.

The latter were well worn, but singularly small for a man of his size and build. The two parties first described were standing directly in front of, and but a few feet distant from where this singular-looking individual lounged.

We have stated that the latter's eyes were expressionless; and yet when the two men mysteriously alluded to Old Electricity, they brightened up with an intelligence and fire, which to an observer would have appeared really startling.

In fact, for one brief instant an expression flitted across his countenance, which completely transformed it, making him look like an entirely different person, so wonderful and remarkable was the change.

IV

BROADWAY BILLY AND JACK HARKAWAY

Munro challenged the house of Beadle with Cap Collier and Old Sleuth. And Beadle came back at him with "Broadway Billy" for a detective; "Jack Harkaway" as a young devil-may-care cosmopolitan; and "Deadwood Dick" for serious business in the West.

I doubt if Broadway Billy ever became as popular as Cap Collier, but the story of "Broadway Billy's Signal Scoop; or, The Strangest Case on Record" is as good as many of the detective novels of the present. That is not extravagant praise. The author was Jesse C. Cowdrick.

Humphrey Haldemyer, the millionaire, has been murdered and robbed. His safe which held all his "papers" and cash was looted, but whoever opened it had sprung a trap, an ingenious little device which was planned to cut off the hand of any meddler. A hand is found near the safe, but it is the hand of a young lady. Broadway Billy, who is called in when the police are in despair, wonders if there is any news of a young lady who has lost her hand.

There is. Miss Julia Donaldson, a young lady of twenty, "talented, accomplished, rich" has had just this misfortune. She is in bed, prostrate, since she has been in a railroad accident at the Grand Central Station. Billy has an interview with her. She is quite sure that she has not been near Mr. Haldemyer's safe; and she doesn't know how her hand got there. Since she has lost it, she feels that she is not exactly responsible for it.

BROADWAY BILLY: HARKAWAY

Billy finds from a "professor" that the blood on the knives of the trap is cat's blood, and he finally arrests Clyde Rosedale, the murdered man's nephew. Clyde had sprung the trap, and killed a cat, in order to have some blood about. He had provided himself with a Negro's hand, which he had procured somewhere — in St. Louis, I think — and was intending to leave that behind. But, unfortunately, it became spoiled. Being, by chance, in the railway wreck, he had luckily picked up Julia's hand and carried it with him to the robbery. When surprised by his uncle at his dishonest work, he had added murder to his other crimes.

Jack Harkaway was a new personage among the dime novels. He originated in England; he was, in a literary sense, the great-grandson of Tom and Jerry, and, on this side of the water, had a nephew in Frank Merriwell.

The author of "Jack Harkaway" was Bracebridge Hemyng. He was called to the bar in London in 1862, and wrote a long list of novels. He brought a new note into the paper-covered fiction of New York.

Consider that the story of "Jack Harkaway in New York; or, The Adventures of the Travelers' Club" begins in London. Lord Maltravers has insulted old Professor Mole, a friend of Jack's, and the two young men hurry over to Calais to fight a duel.

At five o'clock he [his second] had Jack up, and they sought the appointed spot, finding Lord Maltravers and his second already there.

In an instant the principals stripped to their shirts and grasped the weapons which were handed them.

The swords were of highly tempered steel, sharply pointed and as pliable as a willow wand.

The sun was just rising in the east, gilding the horizon with its burning rays. A few fishing-smacks lay in the offing. The tide was on the turn, and the wavelets plashed mournfully on the sand, as if singing a requiem.

"*En garde!*" cried Maltravers.

Jack placed himself in position. His right arm and knee advanced, and his left hand by his side.

The swords clashed as they crossed each other, and recovering, the duelists watched carefully for an opening.

Lord Maltravers lunged in *carte,* but his thrust was delicately foiled by his opponent, who parried it skillfully.

A long strip of plaster hid the cut on his lordship's face, which was ghastly white and terribly in earnest.

For some minutes they fenced with the adroitness of veteran swordsmen, neither gaining the slightest advantage, though a hectic spot which appeared on Maltravers' face indicated that his mind was less at ease than Jack's.

Suddenly Jack ceased to act on the defensive and became the aggressor, breaking down his lordship's guard and pinking him slightly in the left arm.

"First blood!" said Harvey; "are you satisfied?"

"Confound it, no. This is a duel to the death," replied Maltravers, his face distorted with passion.

"As you please," replied Jack.

Again they faced one another, the wounded man having hastily tied a piece of his shirtsleeve round his arm.

The swords clashed in the bright morning sunshine, which every moment became brighter.

In vain Maltravers strove to injure his enemy. Each thrust was parried and he panted with exertion, while tears of impotent rage started to his eyes.

"Ha! I have you now," he exclaimed, as the point of his rapier touched Jack's breast.

"Not quite," replied Jack, who threw himself back, instantly recovered, and lunging in *tierce,* sent his weapon through the left shoulder of the nobleman.

Maltravers staggered; he leant upon his sword, which snapped in half, and he sunk upon his knees, his face convulsed with pain.

This is far removed from "Seth Jones." It sounds rather more like Ouida. Yet Jack Harkaway was a popular and successful character in ten-cent fiction, and one gentleman of my acquaintance remembers him as

his favorite hero, in that era when bustles were fashionable.

V

DEADWOOD DICK

In 1884, when Mr. Blaine and Governor Cleveland were
contesting the presidency, there rode into the lives of the
readers of dime novels probably the most celebrated of
their Western heroes. He was a character in the first
number of "Beadle's Pocket Library," — mean little
pamphlets which sold at five cents each.

Munro had published the stories of the most celebrated of the detectives, but Beadle and Adams, not
long before their decline, showed their vigor when
they published this series by Edward L. Wheeler. It
was not his first novel, but never again in all his list of
alliterations — Rosebud Rob, Photograph Phil, Sierra
Sam, High Hat Harry, Omaha Oll, or Nobby Nick —
did he ever chance upon a name so felicitous or a character so appealing to his readers as that of Deadwood
Dick.

In November, 1928, on the day when Governor Smith
and Mr. Hoover went before the nation for a decision,
the newspapers recorded that Richard W. Clark, the

original, as they asserted, of Deadwood Dick, had arrived in Chicago by airplane. He was on his way from Rapid City, South Dakota, to Washington, to call on the President. There is a far-away resemblance between the pictures of the old frontiersman, aged eighty-two, and the drawings of the young desperado of the eighties, in Mr. Wheeler's stories. I fancy that this distant resemblance is all that obtains between the career of Richard Clark and Deadwood Dick.

The *Evening Sun* of New York, about 1891, printed an article on the hero of fiction, Deadwood Dick, in which it is said that Beadle and Adams had published the first story about him as early as 1877,[1] and that eighty separate books had been printed to recount his adventures, and those of Dick, Junior. All of them — like most of the dime novels — had been reprinted in England.

The *Sun* also said that Mr. Victor was an admirer of the tales, but that he had insisted on making their language less sulphurous, and in drying up some of the "torrents of liquor" which flowed through them.

In the first story a person known as Fearless Frank rescues a maiden of seventeen from the Sioux chieftain, Sitting Bull. This red man has so far forgotten the noble

---

[1] This discrepancy in dates may mean that Dick first appeared in the Beadles' weekly paper.

traditions of his people, as to strip the girl to the waist and have her flogged. But Fearless Frank persuades the chief to release her, and "soon he had the satisfaction of seeing her once more clothed properly" — which, of course, was the really important thing.

When Deadwood Dick appears, he is described as

a youth of an age somewhere between sixteen and twenty, trim and compactly built with a preponderance of muscular development and animal spirits; broad and deep of chest, with square, iron-cast shoulders; limbs small yet like bars of steel, and with a grace of position in the saddle rarely equalled; he made a fine picture for an artist's brush or a poet's pen.

Only one thing marred the captivating beauty of the picture.

His form was clothed in a tight-fitting habit of buckskin, which was colored a jetty black and presented a striking contrast to anything one sees as a garment in the wild far West. And this was not all, either. A broad black hat was slouched down over his eyes; he wore a thick black veil over the upper portion of his face, through the eye-holes of which there gleamed a pair of orbs of piercing intensity, and his hands, large and knotted, were hidden in a pair of kid gloves of a light color.

The "Black Rider" he might have been justly termed, for his thoroughbred steed was as black as coal, but we have not seen fit to call him such — his name is Dead-wood Dick, and let that suffice for the present.

He often utters "a wild sardonic laugh . . . a terrible, blood-curdling laugh." He defeats his enemies, and prevails everywhere, except that he cannot induce his female counterpart, Calamity Jane, to marry him. She refuses, although "he was still masked, well-armed, and looking every inch a Prince of the Road." So:

Calamity Jane is still in the Hills. . . .

And, grim and uncommunicative there roams through the country of gold a youth in black, at the head of a bold lawless gang of road-riders, who from his un-equalled daring has won and rightly deserves the name of — Deadwood Dick, Prince of the Road.

He continues to roam for many years. And now, if we accept Mr. Clark, he roams by airplane. A newspaper pointed out, with good-natured irony, that the airmen daily take greater risks and show more quiet courage than all the heroes and villains of the dime novels.

This is not said in disparagement of Mr. Wheeler. Of all the writers of his school, there is none whose lan-guage more fully satisfies our notions of how things should be said. Listen to this speech, made during a hold-up, in "The Frontier Detective; or, Sierra Sam's Scheme":

"Old gent, it cannot avail you anything to hesitate. The stage is covered by enough rifles to riddle it, and if you don't hand over your cash, chattels an' jewelry, why, I shall most certainly have the horses shot, and you will be even more at our mercy. Then you will perhaps find that Lady Lil, the road-agent, holds the winning hand!" [1]

[1] In the preceding paragraph I used the old Americanism "hold-up," which was good enough for Deadwood Dick, and is good enough for me. He told his victims, when he wished them to raise their hands on high, to "Hold 'em up!" or "Put up your hands!" Who foisted the Australianism, "stick-up," upon the language of American banditry? Even our gunmen are now *said* to shout: "Stick 'em up!" Some newspaper reporter evidently read Mr. Hornung's stories of "Stingaree," the Australian bushranger, and lacked the sturdy patriotism to hang on to our own slang. Why must we, who boast of our slang, constantly borrow from the English and Australians?

PART III

OLD AGE

I

THE MENACE OF RESPECTABILITY

WHEN did dime novels commence to dodder down the hill into old age? When did their arteries harden and respectability set in? When did they cease to be a moral menace and become a literary curiosity?

Different dates might be set. It could be June 28, 1899, when a senior at Harvard College discussed them in an address at Commencement.[1] Or it could be in 1922, when Doctor Frank O'Brien's gift to the New York Public Library, of fourteen hundred Beadles and other publications, was boldly put on show. Men still young who gazed at this exhibition could easily remember when the librarian of a public library would show more cordiality to a *cobra de capello* within his doors than to a dime novel. When another large set of them toured the country and were exhibited in libraries everywhere, there was the end of an old superstition. An ancient bugaboo had perished.

Nevertheless, two famous characters, Nick Carter and Frank Merriwell, and a number of lesser ones — Old

[1] "The Degeneration of the Dime Novel," by Robert Peabody Bellows. Reprinted in *The Writer*, July, 1899.

King Brady, Young Wild West, Frank Reade, Diamond Dick, and those real bandits, the James boys — bridged the period between the old and the new and make it hard to draw the line. Probably not one of them was, in a strict sense, a character in a dime novel. They belonged to the "nickel libraries" or to the boys' weeklies of varying titles.

There was also a return to virtue. Nick Carter was as good as Rollo or as an Oliver Optic boy — though perhaps not goody-good. He never drank, smoked a cigarette, or swore. And Frank Merriwell was a school and college hero. Old Cap Collier, as we have seen, although the shield and buckler of the innocent, and the terror of the criminal classes, himself descended into sin. He gambled and he drank; I am not sure but that he smoked.

II

NICK CARTER

Nick Carter (whose stories are published by the firm of Street and Smith) went everywhere, did everything, and was a universal hero. In a thousand years, he may very well have become a solar myth. His sponsors and cre-

No. 710   AUG. 6, 1910   5 CENTS

NICK CARTER

REG. U.S. PAT. OFF.

THE STOCKBRIDGE AFFAIR

Nick rolled away the heavy desk, and, lifting the flap cut in the rug, together with the trap in the floor, he shot the light into the darkness below.

ators have been dying, one by one, and each time a death was recorded, there has been renewed discussion as to the share this man had in writing the stories in the "Nick Carter Library."

It is held that John Russell Coryell suggested the name for Nick and wrote a few of the novels at the start. Frederick van Rensselaer Dey and Eugene T. Sawyer wrote many of the hundreds which followed. The name was used "back in the 70's" by "a number of publishers." [1]

Mr. Eugene Sawyer (who died in 1924 at the age of seventy-eight, in San José) was interviewed by Gelett Burgess more than twenty-five years ago. [2] Mr. Burgess found, at the city editor's desk of a San José newspaper, a genial, sadly smiling gentleman, whose greatest care, outside his newspaper work, was for his geraniums. In fact, the picture of Mr. Sawyer, with his spectacles, makes him look like the principal of a high school.

"Oh, I have retired long since," said Mr. Sawyer. "As I explained, I did it partly for the fun of it and the love of excitement. As to pay, I used to get fifty dollars apiece for the Nick Carters, and they ran to about 25,000 words.

[1] The *Sun*, New York, November 1, 1924. *New York Times*, October 30, 1924. For a charming account of Mr. Coryell, see "The Birth of Nick Carter" in The *Bookman* (N. Y.) July, 1929.

[2] The *Bookman* (New York) August, 1902.

The 'Log Cabin' novels were twice as long, or 50,000 words, and I got $100 apiece, so the pay averaged two dollars a thousand words. I 'Americanized' one of the Nick Carters from Gaboriau in three days once, and once I turned out three 50,000-word novels in a month. Then I did serials for the *New York Weekly*. I have written about seventy-five novels in all.

"I fancy I revolutionized the opening of the dime novel. Writers for the magazines have learned how necessary it is to begin the plot with the first word, and do it perhaps more artistically, but it's the same principle. Here are some of my beginnings. For instance, in 'Ramon Aranda, the California Detective,' I start:

" 'We will have the money, or she shall die!' " or, in another one I thought rather striking:

" 'Swear the defendant!'

"And in 'The Dead Man's Hand' the opening line was this:

" 'It is a case of mysterious disappearance, Mr. Carter!'

"Perhaps my chief inspiration was old Ned Buntline, who was really the first one to write 'penny dreadfuls' and the inventor of the 'dime novel.' He made Buffalo Bill famous, but he was vastly more picturesque himself than Bill or than any of his own characters.

"The fastest work I ever did," Mr. Sawyer said, "was once when I got an order by wire from Street and Smith, saying that one of their regular writers had failed them, and asking if I could send them a story of 60,000 words in four days. Of course I accepted. And that, too, was in the days of longhand, before typewriters were common. As usual, I procrastinated, and two days had elapsed before I thought about the story. Then I locked myself into my room and began, writing in lead pencil, while my wife copied my work in ink. I didn't eat or sleep, living on coffee alone, till the novel was completed, in about sixty hours. In order to have the manuscript reach the publishers on time, I had to have it in the post-office at noon, and I caught that mail with something less than a minute to spare."

"You must have travelled a good deal, Mr. Sawyer," I said, "for from your stories I see you are familiar with New York and the East."

"I was in New York for four days in 1865," he replied, "and upon that brief acquaintance I founded my scenes."

Frederick van Rensselaer Dey, in poverty and despair, shot himself in his room in the Hotel Broztell, New York, in April, 1922. He wrote books under his own name, and as Varick Vanardy, as Bertha M. Clay and as Marion Gilmore. It is said that he also wrote "more than 1000 'Nick Carter' novelettes, some forty million words in all. . . ." [1]

"I never in my life wrote a 'Nick Carter' that I would be ashamed to read to a Bible class," he used to say.

And this seems justified when we read how decent Nick was to the Mikado of Japan. Shortly before the outbreak of the war with Russia, so we read in the *Nick Carter Weekly,* the Emperor called in the American detective to find out which one of his great nobles was betraying State secrets.

The Mikado received Nick Carter, as the colored picture shows, dressed in his robes, somewhat as in the opera named for him. But quite informally, and with perfectly affable manners. Later in the day, they went into private conference. The author says:

At three o'clock that afternoon the Mikado of Japan entered the room in the summer palace that had been assigned to the detective.

Nick, who had long since risen, and was therefore now thoroughly rested from the fatigues of his journey, was waiting to receive him, and was pleased as well as surprised at the punctuality of the emperor.

[1] *Newark News,* quoted in *The Literary Digest,* May 20, 1922.

Evidently with the intention of putting the detective thoroughly at his ease, the Mikado was attired in the costume of an American, so that he appeared as any gentleman might have done who had come there merely for the purposes of an interview.

Once more he shook hands with his guest with the utmost cordiality.

"I am glad to see that you are rested after your journey, Mr. Carter," he said. "I hope that you have been well attended since your arrival."

"Perfectly, sir."

"Before we begin the regular business of this interview, I wish to impress upon you my wish that we meet always on the basis of friends and that all needless formalities be omitted between us. An emperor can have but few friends, and I would consider it a privilege to count you as one of mine. Whenever we are fortunate enough to find ourselves alone together or only in the presence of Ten-Ichi, we will understand each other much better if we meet on common ground."

"I appreciate this courtesy, sir, more than I can say," replied Nick.

"It is even a greater privilege to me than it is to you, Mr. Carter, although you may not see it in that light."

Nick bowed.

III

YALE'S GREATEST HERO

To the experienced dime novelist, William G. Patten, the firm of Street and Smith proposed the character who was afterwards named Frank Merriwell.[1]

This was in 1895. The publishers saw a waning interest — at that time — in the Western yarn, and desired a light-hearted hero, with a light-hearted name (like Jack Harkaway) who should be thoroughly American, and who might go through school, military academy and college. There was to be much athletic adventure in the saga, since there was everywhere a growing interest in college sports.

The name of "Burt L. Standish" was chosen for the author, or authors, of the stories, so that they might go right on, by other hands, if Mr. Patten were struck by lightning or anything. He was to do twenty thousand words a week.

It was a success; the first number appeared April 18, 1896, and sold out immediately. The *Tip Top Weekly*

---

[1] "Man Merriwell." By James M. Cain. *Saturday Evening Post,* June 11, 1927.

was chiefly devoted to Frank Merriwell and his adventures.

Mr. Patten said that there had to be comic characters, but that you cannot give boys real humor. They do not understand anything but slapstick. They also enjoy characters like Harry Rattleton, who always said, "I seel filly, I mean I feel silly." Boys think that very funny. Other devices were Carl Hans Dunnerwurst, the Dutch boy, and Ephraim Gallup, the lanky Yankee boy, who every time things began to get hot, would moan, "I wisht I was to hum on the farm."

"Frank was the great boy at Yale," wrote Mr. Cain. "He made the football team every year, and won all the Harvard games single-handed in the last minute of play."

When Frank graduated, as he had to do sometime, his author and publishers were in a hole. How was he to keep going? And what was to be done with the circulation of one hundred and eight thousand per week?

To answer the question they invented Dick Merriwell, but he was a "dreadful flop."

IV

ALL THE MANLY VIRTUES

THE boys' weeklies, which were very popular in the eighteen nineties and nineteen hundreds, included *Work and Win,* with its hero, Fred Fearnot; the *Wild West Weekly,* with "Young Wild West" and his "Arietta"; *Secret Service,* with "Old King Brady" and "Young K. B."; *Pluck and Luck;* and the *Frank Reade Weekly,* with Frank's electrified inventions. All these were published by Frank Tousey. The "Old King Brady" stories are attributed to Francis Worcester Doughty, who, curiously, was the author of works on numismatics and archaeology.

Street and Smith published *Diamond Dick Jr. Weekly; Young Broadbrim; Tip Top Weekly;* the *Brave and Bold Series; Boys of Liberty Library;* and the *Log Cabin Library,* with the stories of Jesse and Frank James.

A parody is sometimes more real than the thing itself. It is at once an exposition and a criticism. No quotation from one of the boys' weeklies could recall them with more accuracy than this passage from George Ade's

PLUCK AND LUCK

COMPLETE STORIES OF ADVENTURE

Issued Weekly—By Subscription $2.50 per year. Entered as Second Class Matter at the New York Post-Office, November 7, 1898, by Frank Tousey.

No. 304.   NEW YORK, MARCH 30, 1904.   Price 5 Cents.

THE BOY SPECULATORS OF BROOKTON
OR, MILLIONAIRES AT NINETEEN.
By ALLYN DRAPER

"You villain! move an inch and I'll brain you!" he cried. He was waving the sandbag over his head with one hand, while clutching the roll of bills with the other.

"YOU VILLAIN! MOVE AN INCH AND I'LL BRAIN YOU!"

"Handsome Cyril; or, The Messenger Boy with the Warm Feet." [1]

"CYRIL!"

"Alexander!"

The two messenger boys clasped hands.

It was on Madison Street — that busy thoroughfare where many streams of humanity meet in whirling vortexes.

The afternoon sun lighted up the features of Cyril Smith, the courageous young messenger boy.

His steel-gray eyes glinted as he gazed at his friend and comrade, Alexander. He had regular features and a regular suit of messenger-boy clothes.

"I hope you are well, Alexander," he said, a smile lighting up his handsome face.

"Oh, yes, quite well, indeed," responded Alexander.

There was a short silence broken only by the continuous uproar of the street. Then Alexander asked: "Where are you going?"

"I am delivering a death message," replied Cyril thoughtfully.

"Well, I must ascertain how the baseball game is progressing," said Alexander, and shaking our hero by the hand he moved away.

"Alexander is a strange youth," said Cyril musingly. "I sometimes think he must be pessimistic."

[1] From "Bang! Bang." By George Ade. J. H. Sears and Company, New York, 1928.

At that moment the shriek of a woman in agony smote upon his ears.

"What is this?" he asked. "A woman in trouble? I must buy an extra and find out what has occasioned this disturbance."

For at that moment the newsboys were shouting the extras which told why the woman had screamed.

Such is life in a great city.

Our hero ran toward the corner.

He saw a beautiful woman struggling in the grasp of a fashionably-attired man.

She was a magnificent creature. Great swirls of raven hair fell in profusion down her back. The alabaster whiteness of her face served to intensify her beauty. She wore a diamond necklace, diamond earrings, and her lily-white hands flashed with precious jewels.

She turned an appealing look at our hero and said: "Oh, sir, save me!"

Bing!

With a well-directed blow Cyril sent the fashionably-dressed man sprawling on the pavement. With the other arm he supported the fainting woman. Then with the other hand he picked up the lace handkerchief which had fallen to the ground and presented it to her with a graceful bow.

"Curse you!" shouted the villain, struggling to his feet. "I shall cause you to rue this deed."

"Coward!" exclaimed Cyril with a curling lip. "How dare you strike this woman?"

"We shall meet again," said Cyril's antagonist, ominously, and with these words he stepped into a carriage and was driven rapidly away.

Our hero now turned his attention to the beautiful creature who reclined in his arms.

"Speak! Speak!" he whispered.

Slowly the glorious eyes opened, and then she asked, in tremulous tones: "Where is he?"

"Gone."

"Where to?"

"That I cannot say, madam," responded Cyril, for though he was only a messenger boy he had been taught to be courteous.

"His name is Rudolf Belmont. He must be followed."

"Yes, madam."

"He has taken the papers which prove that I am the real owner of the Belmont estate."

A shudder passed through our hero's frame. Then recovering himself he said: "Madam, I will follow that villain and recover the papers."

"Oh, thank you," she said, and for a few minutes she wept softly.

Finally she lifted her tear-stained face and said: "Summon a conveyance and if you are ever in need of a friend come to this number," saying which she gave Cyril an engraved card and offered him a purse containing gold.

"No, madam," said Cyril, with dignity. "I will not take your money. My salary is sufficient to permit me to live in comparative luxury."

V

READERS' RECOLLECTIONS

Six or seven years ago, in writing an article for a weekly periodical about the O'Brien collection of dime novels, I began with this sentence, which at the time I thought rather clever:

Arithmeticians might calculate that if all the switches, hickory sticks, straps, hair-brush backs, and other instruments of torture which have been applied by angry parents to the readers of dime novels . . . should be placed "end to end" they would reach from William Street in New York, where the novels used to be published, to Cooperstown where Erastus Beadle ended his days.

In writing this, I was probably acting under the obsession which makes us accept traditions about boyhood without stopping to think whether they were true, in our own experience or knowledge. Comic writers and artists are forever representing boys at "the old swimming hole" tying up one boy's clothes, wetting the knots, and then shouting "Chaw bacon!" while the wretch struggles with the knots. How many have ever seen it happen?

It occurred to me, while I was writing this book, to

test the truth of the hundreds of beatings and spankings supposed to have been inflicted by Father, in the woodshed, upon readers of dime novels.

Although I think the sender of a questionnaire the most loathly type of nuisance, I did venture to ask a number of friends and acquaintances, together with a few others whom I have not the pleasure of knowing personally, one or two questions about dime novels. These were briefly: Did you read them? Did you know of anybody getting punished for reading them?

I was prompted to do this by the very amusing experience, written before I sent out the letters, of my friend, Percy Waxman. The profound (temporary) effect of Deadwood Dick upon a small boy in Australia, seemed to me entertaining, and possibly significant.[1]

The letters from my courteous correspondents follow.

Booth Tarkington says that he was "forbidden by his parents to read dime novels" but that he managed to do so constantly by concealing them inside a copy of an approved book, for instance, "Pilgrim's Progress," etc. He did most of this stolen reading under sofas or the

---

[1] What it signifies, I do not know. But it does not do to write a book, without finding something or other significant.

piano, but preferably in the sawdust box in the stable. He was never punished when caught, but he was scolded and encouraged to read history and standard works.

It should be remembered that Mr. Tarkington's "Penrod" (also in the sawdust box) was engaged, at his first appearance, in trying to write a dime novel. His efforts illustrate a boy's unconscious parody of this kind of story. Here are a few extracts:

Mr. Wilson reched for his gun but our hero had him covred and soon said Well I guess you don't come any of that on me my freind

Well what makes you so sure about it sneered the other bitting his lip so savageley that the blood ran You are nothing but a comon Roadagent any way and I do not propose to be bafled by such, Ramorez laughed at this and kep Mr Wilson covred by his ottomatick

Soon the two men were struggling together in the deathroes but soon Mr Wilson got him bound and gaged his mouth and went away for awhile leavin our hero, it was dark and writhd at his bonds writhing on the floor wile the rats came out of their holes and bit him and vernim got all over him from the floor of that helish spot but soon he manged to push the gag out of his mouth with the end of his toungeu and got all bonds off

Soon Mr. Wilson came back to tant him with his helpless condition flowed by his gang of detectives and they said Oh look at Ramorez sneering at his plight and tanted him with his helpless condition because Ramorez had put the bonds back sos he would look the same but could throw them off him when he wanted to Just look at him now sneered they. To hear him talk you would have thought he was hot stuff and they said Look at him now, him that was going to do so much. Oh I would not like to be in his fix

Soon Harold got mad at this and jumped up with blasing eyes throwin off his bonds like they were air Ha Ha sneered he I guess you better not talk so much next time. Soon there flowed another awful struggle and siezin his ottomatick back from Mr Wilson he shot two of the detectives through the heart Bing Bing went the ottomatick and two more went to meet their Maker only two detectives left now and so he stabbed one and the scondrel went to meet his Maker for now our hero was fighting for his very life. It was dark in there now for night had falen and a terrible view met the eye Blood was just all over everything and the rats were eatin the dead men.

Soon our hero manged to get his back to the wall for he was fighting for his very life now and shot Mr Wilson through the abodmen Oh said Mr Wilson you — — — [The dashes are Penrod's]

Mr Wilson stagered back vile oaths soilin his lips for he was in pain Why you — — you sneered he I will get you yet — — you Harold Ramorez

The remainin scondrel had an ax which he came near our heros head with but missed him and remand

[225]

stuck in the wall Our heros amumition was exhaused
what was he to do, the remanin scondrel would get his
ax lose so our hero sprung forward and bit him till his
teeth met in the flech for now our hero was fighting for
his very life. At this the remanin scondrel also cursed
and swore vile oaths Oh sneered he —— —— you Harold
Ramorez what did you bite me for Yes sneered Mr. Wilson also and he has shot me in the abodmen too . . .

Robert Bridges, editor of *Scribner's Magazine,* says:

"My greatest sin was Jack Harkaway and his adventures. They could not be classed as dime novels, and I
am afraid that the present generation of boys would
laugh at the tameness of Jack's adventures.

"I must have read Ned Buntline, but I don't recall
anything about it.

"The two magazines that I associated with boyhood
were *The Little Corporal,* edited, I think, by Emily
Huntington Miller, and published in Chicago; and *Our
Young Folks* which contained, as I remember, Aldrich's
'Story of a Bad Boy' and Mayne Reid's 'Afloat in the
Forest; or, A Voyage among the Treetops.'

"When Roosevelt was planning his South American
trip, I told him that all I knew about it came from that
story, and I only recalled the hero floating down the
river with a life-preserver made of coconut shells. The

Colonel immediately outlined the principal characters in the story and chortled with delight as he recalled what he had not read for probably forty years."

This is from Samuel Hopkins Adams:

"Dime novels? Of course they were taboo, strictly so. To be a devotee of this kind of reading was as bad as smoking the surreptitious cigarette or going to a 'leg show' of the Black Crook variety.

"Brought up a minister's son — albeit, a very liberal-minded minister — I was not supposed to know anything about that sort of literature, but I can recall reading circles gathered in the barn on rainy days when some adventurous spirit of the Third Ward crowd would produce one of these thrillers and read from it while the rest of us shoved for favored positions near him where we could see the illustrations. There was one taboo more rigid than dime novels, however; the *Police Gazette*.

"Here is proof of the ten-centers' contraband character. For years I have been collecting antiques from the garrets, cellars, and store-rooms of my rural locality (Central New York), but I have yet to come upon one of the old dime novels with the lurid-hued covers in paper.

Well would I like to! As you know, they are precious trove for the collector. It may be argued that, being flimsy pamphlets they were highly destructible and would logically be the first type of publication to disappear. This will not do. Much earlier paper-covered prints of an improving kind are plentiful still; almost any old, rural bookcase will have a few, telling of little Willie's cutting the firewood for Grandpa, or pointing a moral from the case of Disobedient Dan who went fishing on Sunday, fell into the lake, and was bitten by a pious-minded pickerel. No; the 'Nick Carter' series and their ilk are rare and precious now because they were confiscated on sight by the censors of an earlier day.

"I can still recall the thrill of an early experience as a reporter when, sent to Brooklyn to write the 'obit' of the deceased president of the Board of Education, I found that he had been a famous dime-novel author under a pseudonym — I've forgotten which; it may have been Nick Carter, himself. His habit of composition was to take ten school pads of the coarsest paper, two-for-a-nickel, and scribble at top speed with a soft pencil for four hours at a stretch, tearing off each sheet and throwing it on the floor as finished, whence an emissary from his publisher gathered it in and bore it off to the printer, unread and uncorrected. When only one pad remained, it was time to slay the villain, rescue the maiden, and close up the plot. How he ever escaped utter confusion of scheme and detail I cannot understand. . . .

"In the early 'nineties one of my fellows on the staff of the New York *Sun,* the famous 'Jersey' Chamberlain — not yet famous — was commissioned to write three dime novels at $100 apiece. Each was to begin 'Bang! Bang! Bang! Three shots rang out on the midnight air,' or words to that effect, the formula being to catch the reader's interest at the first onslaught. I believe he did only one and then quit, because he had exhausted all the exciting details. This proved him an amateur; the same plot, *mutatis mutandis,* would have served for all three. C. C. Tyler, then of the *World,* was credited on Park Row with the authorship of a number of these works of art, issued by a Bowery publisher whose name I cannot recall. He was supposed to take a day off every fortnight and finish one in that time. I believe that the late Saqui Smith served an apprenticeship at the same trade before he undertook more ambitious fiction.

"If I am not mistaken, by this time the bright-colored covers had vanished; but perhaps it was only my interest that had paled."

Wallace Irwin says this:

"As a matter of fact, I was raised in a tough mining camp where life itself was so dime-novelish that dime novels were (if you'll excuse the pun) no dime-novelty to the Irwin boys.

"However, in literary form, they did creep in and somehow get themselves read while our parents looked the other way. In spite of our daily experience with the tough side of the Rockies, we were secretly fascinated by Buffalo Bill. Nick Carter seemed rather tame, as I remember. Once — and I can't remember the title of the classic — I was scared bright blue by a picture of robed figures holding a victim over some sort of blazing pit. The caption read: 'In the golden coffin he shall be burned alive there, said the Father Spirit menacingly.'

"I never heard of a real dime novel spanking. If the parental shingle was used upon my fellow gangsters, after a late session with Jesse James, I know nothing of it. My mother used diplomacy, and I lost my taste for single-line thrillers at an early age."

Percy Waxman, associate editor of *The Pictorial Review,* writes:

"What a fascination the Wild and Woolly West has

SIXTH EDITION.

Copyrighted in 1879 by BEADLE AND ADAMS.

Vol. IV. Single Number. BEADLE AND ADAMS, PUBLISHERS, No. 98 WILLIAM STREET, NEW YORK. Price, 5 Cents. No. 86.

DANDY ROCK, THE MAN FROM TEXAS.

A WILD ROMANCE OF THE LAND OF GOLD.

BY G. WALDO BROWNE.

Five, ten, fifteen minutes wore away, and still the cougar had not left his perch, neither had the gleaming eyes left for even a moment their prey.

"NEITHER HAD THE GLEAMING EYES LEFT
FOR EVEN A MOMENT THEIR PREY."

(See page 266)

always had for foreigners! And what weird ideas about 'America' motion pictures are spreading before their pop-eyed audiences all over the world. In a sense, I suppose, these Western films are the illogical successors of the dime novels of former days and I only hope that the small boys who sit excitedly in front of them in foreign lands get as lasting a thrill as I did from the paper-covered literature of my early youth.

"I lived in Melbourne, Australia, and long before I had reached the age of twelve I was familiar (in a way) with many phases of life in America and with much of its early pioneer background, almost entirely from what I had absorbed from dime novels. Furthermore, those colorful volumes gave me an intense desire to visit the United States and meet as many of its remarkable inhabitants as possible. A country that could produce such unusually interesting men and women as those who figured in its books could not be overlooked.

"I must have been about ten or eleven when a dime novel first fell into my eager hands and the frenzied rapture that the poets speak of is a pale anaemic thing compared with the maddened joy of that initiation into American literature. The book contained 32 pages and dealt with the glorious exploits of a noble son of the

West named Deadwood Dick. A more versatile, ingenious, courageous, and handsome hero has never
yet appeared on my horizon. The man existed solely
for the doing of good in a most picturesque manner.
Dick had the good luck to possess a remarkably capable
feminine partner in the thwarting of villainy named
Calamity Jane. And he needed her, all right, to help
thwart the diabolical depredations of a cur named Piute
Dave (whose name gave me much difficulty to pronounce). This inhuman wretch, by a detestable stroke
of deception, captured Dick in the very first chapter
and tears of sympathy filled my eyes when I read how
Dave and his gang hanged Dick, riddled his body with
bullets from their six-shooters, placed his body in a
sack filled with stones and then, with ghoulish glee, the
dastards hurled the whole grim package from the dizzy
height of a yawning precipice into the boiling cauldron
of a stream several hundred feet below!

"I was horror-stricken to read of this cold-blooded
treatment of so noble a hero and I couldn't quite make
out what the rest of the book could possibly deal with,
when the leading character, after whom the volume was
named, had been so summarily dealt with in Chapter
One. However, on I read, hoping that Calamity Jane

might be able (in a girlish way, of course) to do something about avenging her pal.

"In Chapter Two a bearded stranger appeared in the gambling hell attached to 'The Bloody Gulch Saloon,' and this unknown proceeded to make things pretty hot for Piute Dave and his dastards — to say nothing of the excitement he gave a panting ten-year-old reader.

"After some of the cleverest outwitting and thwarting of devilish plots and plans you ever heard of, this bearded stranger eventually rounded up, not only Piute Dave himself, but his whole gang, and turned them over to the Sheriff. Then, and not till then, did he remove his beard, and who do you think he turned out to be? You'd never guess in a million years, so I'd better put you out of your misery. *It was Deadwood Dick!* He hadn't been killed at all! All the time he had been lying helpless in the sack, he had been unconscious and it just needed the cold chill of the river-water for all his faculties to shift from neutral to third, so to speak. When Dick revealed himself to the gang they couldn't have been half as astonished as I was at his miraculous escape. Later on, when I learned that Deadwood Dick 'ran' through an entire series I didn't care what happened to him in the first few chapters of whatever 'number' I was reading.

I knew he'd reappear safe and sound in the final roundup, with all the villains either swinging from handy trees or in the hands of some rough but law-abiding sheriff.

"Not being sophisticated enough to know that I was reading pernicious literature, I made no attempt to hide my first 'Deadwood Dick' from my family and great was my surprise when a much older brother told me never to bring another one of 'those things' into the house. I was positively shocked at this blasphemous request, but as my brother was very 'high-brow' and intellectually-inclined I felt instinctively that he didn't know the real inwardness of such things, anyhow, and the only notice I took of his astonishing warning was to keep my Deadwood Dicks to myself ever after, and prevent them from falling under the gaze of non-be-lievers.

"My chief pal and fellow-addict at that time was the son of the headmaster of a famous Public School in Melbourne, a merry young rip who was just as keen on dime novels as I was. One evening, while visiting his home, I saw his father seated in front of the fire reading a little paper-covered book and my heart gave a great thump of delight when I discovered that it was one of our Deadwood Dick series. Without a word of explanation I dashed from the room and ran all the way home to find my high-brow brother.

" 'You told me,' I fairly panted the words out, 'that those books I read are bad and that they have a wicked influence on boys.'

" 'So they do,' said my literary mentor.

" 'Well, you must be wrong,' I said triumphantly. 'Dr. Morrison reads them and if they're good enough for him they're good enough for me.'

"Vain was the attempt to explain to me that the reverend doctor read them as a temporary relaxation. I just knew he read them because they were the finest books in the world.

"One natural result of my interest in the 'Deadwood Dick' series was the formation of a secret club. With the customary modesty of youth I appointed myself its head, and on dark nights paraded around the neighborhood in a 'get-up' that approximated my hero's as much as the contents of several wardrobes permitted. Not being able to get possession of a bowie knife, I had to be satisfied with a fruit-knife, thrust into a scabbard that had once been my mother's spectacle-case. I, of course, was Deadwood Dick. My friend, the dominie's son, was Sunflower Sam, while lesser lights played lesser parts. Our greatest cause for grief was that there was no girl of our acquaintance fit to be Calamity Jane.

"A young financial genius in our neighborhood who had no real love of Western Life conceived the idea of a lending library, so having secured the financial backing of his father he purchased a dozen copies of our favorite series and allowed us addicts to pay him threepence a week for the privilege of reading as many books as we could devour. Think of a kid of twelve thinking up a scheme like that! By now no doubt he is either an Australian banking magnate or a well-hated owner of a million second mortgages.

"And as for the pernicious influence of such books that my brother was so fearful of, well, it depends (like the influence of all books) on the reader. All I can say is that after devouring 'Deadwood Dicks' for three or four years I lived to become a Sunday-school teacher, an abstainer from alcohol and tobacco, while the nearest I've ever come to cultivating the practice of murder is a slight tendency to procrastination (see De Quincey)."

From Herbert Asbury, author of "Up from Methodism"; "Hatrack," and "The Gangs of New York":

[236]

"I read dime novels whenever I could get them as a boy, and never met with any opposition from my father. Indeed it is my recollection that he read them himself; I recall that the first ones I ever read were dog-eared and scuffed, and had been around the house for many years before I came upon them and tasted their delights. My grandfather, himself a forty-niner and with several years' experience among the Indians, was always violently opposed to the novels that purported to describe life among the red-skins, for he said that they were packed with lies and were unfair to the Indian. But he always read the ones that dealt with life in the great cities.

"I recall the nickel libraries, such as 'Tip Top Weekly,' 'Secret Service Weekly,' 'Diamond Dick,' and 'Old Sleuth,' much more vividly than the dime novels, although we used to spend our savings for the latter and for the ten- and twenty-five-cent novels about Frank and Dick Merriwell. The nickel libraries were not in such favor at our house. My father permitted us to read them during the summer, but when winter came the practice was stopped, on the ground that it interfered with studies. But of course that never really kept us from reading them. We used to have a box sunk in a hole

[237]

in the barn floor in which we kept our books, and spent hours in the loft, flat on stomach, poring over the adventures of Diamond Dick, the Liberty Boys of Seventy-six, Frank Merriwell, Ben Bright and other heroes. We used to take them to school and read them during recitation and study periods, hiding them in the big geographies and other books which we were supposed to be studying.

"Those nickel booklets were much more popular when I was a boy than the regular dime novels: I remember distinctly that Pelty's Book Store in my home town of Farmington, Missouri, used to sell great piles of them, and that on the day of issue every boy who had a nickel would have one. I think that the Frank Merriwells were the most popular, perhaps because they dealt almost entirely with athletics.

"I never heard of but one boy being whipped for reading dime or nickel novels, and he was whipped for almost everything he did. His father was a very devout churchman, and permitted him to read hardly anything except the Bible and his Sunday-school lessons. I once saw this boy licked for reading the funny papers on a Sunday."

George Ade writes:

"Of course, I was devoted to the nickel library. The dime novel was just a little ahead of my time, although I read a great many issues. . . . Last year John Mc-Cutcheon and I compiled some burlesques of the old nickel library and published them in a volume called 'BANG! BANG!', issued by Sears and Company in New York. In the preface to the volume I explained that I had always been interested in the nickel library or those specimens of 'the haymow literature which was denounced by parents and encouraged by boys from the time of Horace Greeley up to the golden age ushered in by the comic strip. The nickel library came after the yellow-back novel, which dealt mostly with smoking tepees, crouching savages and trappers who were deadly with the rifle and wore fringe on their buckskin suits. One reason for the enduring popularity of the nickel library was that it could be spread open inside of a school geography and entirely concealed from any teacher who did not approach from the rear.' "

Alfred F. Goldsmith, the book dealer, and Whitman bibliographer, says that he procured a large copy of Longfellow's "Tales of a Wayside Inn." He tore out the leaves, and when the parental eyes were on him used this hollow sham to conceal the copy of "Old Cap Collier" which he was actually reading. The fact was recently recalled to his mind when he found the gutted copy of Longfellow.

Marc Connelly, author of "Beggar on Horseback" and other plays:

"Dime novels did not circulate in my set. However, our parents referred to the nickel weeklies we read as 'dime novels.' I spent a good part of my ninth, tenth and eleventh years explaining the difference, but it never did much good. Occasionally I found myself in possession of a real dime novel; I believe my acquaintance with Nick Carter and his faithful Chick, came exclusively through that high-priced medium. It was a pleasant acquaintance, but (could it have been the difference in price?) they never fascinated me as did those two detectives of the five cent libraries, 'Old' and 'Young King Brady.' They enchanted me. Young King Brady was Old King Brady's adopted son, I believe. When they weren't disguised — and they never were on the covers — they looked like two stern deacons, with their black Fedora hats, Prince Albert coats and

SECRET SERVICE

OLD AND YOUNG KING BRADY, DETECTIVES.

No. 269. NEW YORK, MARCH 18, 1904. Price 5 Cents.

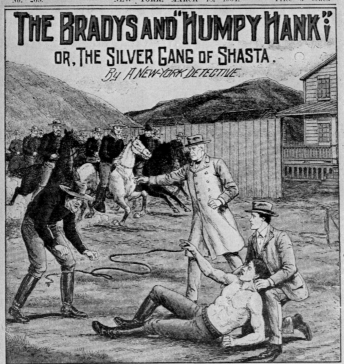

THE BRADYS AND "HUMPY HANK"
OR, THE SILVER GANG OF SHASTA.
By A NEW-YORK DETECTIVE.

Barton's eyes turned, met those of Humpy Hank, and he cried in a terrible voice: "You here, murderer! I have roamed the world over to find you, and avenge the death of Janet Ward!" The Bradys were given a shock.

"YOU HERE, MURDERER!"

freshly pressed trousers. I was always impressed by their agreements to meet at 'a certain hotel' or 'a certain restaurant.' There was always a thrill for me in those mysterious phrases. Years later I thanked the gods of accident when I learned that the man who wrote them was a California school teacher who had never been in New York, where their activities, of course, centered.

"Another hero was Young Wild West. Each week I had to reconcile myself to his long golden locks. I think I'm still a little in love with his sweetheart, Arietta. She was a wonderful sharp-shooter, almost as accurate as her lover, but the most guileless girl that ever got into a villain's clutches. Although she was very beautiful I don't believe anyone ever threatened her with a fate worse than death. Indians merely wanted to torture her and white rascals might tie her to the branch of a tree which in five minutes would go down into the canyon when the fuse reached the powder under the roots, but they had respect for a woman's honor. I don't believe Young Wild West ever even kissed her. He just spent his life rescuing her.

"I liked the adventures but had no particular affection for the personalities of Frank and Dick Merriwell. Burt

[241]

L. Standish moralized a bit as I remember and that probably lukewarmed my loyalty. It was pleasant to see the bullies whipped, though.

"The popularity of the Alger titles, I suppose, prompted the creation of the 'Pluck and Luck' and similarly titled series. I thought they were great, but I can't remember anything about them except the general title and the fact that they had a different hero each week.

"The 'Liberty Boys' held my interest for a year or two. They were stories of the Revolution and proved conclusively that all Tories were dogs.

"But Frank Reade, Jr., that Jules Verne of the nickel novels, was my writer of writers. I can still see his young inventor taking across the African desert that marvelous electric wagon. When savages got inside the wagon the explorers simply stood on glass chairs and pulled electrocuting switches. He also found a continent up behind the North Pole that sent me into my teens with a terrifying thrill.

"We used to prop our books against the larger pages of Frye's Geography with considerable success, when Miss Daft of the Market Street School, McKeesport, Pennsylvania, wasn't looking. If she came down the aisle, all you had to do was turn a page and there you were reading all about mountain ranges."

Richardson Wright, editor of *House and Garden,* says: "I never did read dime novels, but my father did — read them on the sly and kept them, so he once told me, in the upper part of the family privy. Whether or not he was ever whipped for reading these books has never been handed down as a family tradition."

Frank Craven, the actor, and author of "The First Year," etc., writes:

"Deadwood Dick was not my favorite as a kid. Nor even Nick Carter or Old Cap Collier.

"*But* The James Boys: 'The James Boys in Missouri'; 'The James Boys in Kansas'; and in fact the whole series of the James Boys were my special delight.

"Met Frank James, back in 1900, in St. Paul and had one of my greatest thrills.

"When I travelled with my mother and father on the road, I was often left at the hotel while they were at the theatre and from the time they left for work until they came home I would read. My favorite spot was the corner of the room facing the door. Then I could give my entire attention to the novel and not be bothered with having to look over my shoulder every minute.

"They were, of course, five cents apiece, and then, if you recall, it was possible to take them to a second-hand book store, where they could be resold at the rate of three or four for a nickel — and there was the price of a new 'James Boys Series.'

"There was a character known as Mysterious Ike; a masked person, who afterwards turned out to be a woman in love with Jesse James; this masked person always turned up in the nick of time, to show Jesse and Frank a short cut through the woods, or an underground passage. The saddest day of my young life was the day Jesse was shot by the Ford Boys, and the series was ended."

Here is an astronomer's experience: Doctor Walter S. Adams, director of the Mount Wilson Observatory:

"I did read dime novels as a boy and usually kept them carefully concealed in the attic. This was not absolutely essential, because my father, although disapproving of them in a general way, did not really consider them as works of the 'Evil One,' to use the current New England expression. At the same time, I think there is little doubt that he would have consigned to the fire any copies he had come across. I do not know from personal knowledge of any boy who was whipped for reading dime novels, but I think it may well have happened in Derry, New Hampshire, in the eighteen eighties. I know of boys who were obliged to read the Bible (almost invariably the Old Testament) for as much as three hours at a time because of having been caught reading secular books on Sunday afternoon. This was one of the great problems of my boyhood — what constituted 'Sunday reading' — and the answers to it were very interesting. Apparently, for example, the religious wars of Europe after the Reformation were suitable, but the Napoleonic campaigns were outside the pale.

"I wish I could tell you more of interest, but apparently the dime novel did not affect either my brother or me to the same extent that they did many boys. Our heroes were much more likely to be historical characters, and I can still remember my enthusiasm over Hannibal when I was ten. There was one person in the town of Derry whose opinion on the dime novel I wish I had. He was a little old man with a white beard, a pillar in the church, and at prayer meetings he always closed his prayers with a request to the Lord to have mercy upon 'the great and wicked city of New York.' This expression became a byword with some of us, but what experience on his part lay back of it I never knew. Every morning when he got out of bed he used to look out over the meadows east of his house to see if the second coming of the Lord was at hand."

Edwin F. Edgett, literary editor of the Boston Evening Transcript, writes:

"What I can tell you about reading dime novels is more negative than positive. I do not think that I ever read a dime novel, that is, the sort of story that Beadle published, in my life. I used to read Oliver Optic, Horatio Alger's stories and the serial stories in *Golden Days* and other boys' papers, but they do not belong quite in the dime novel class. Yet in a way, the dime novel was a part of my boyhood life. You may remember that they were liberally displayed in the windows of the periodical stores, and I don't think that I ever passed one without stopping to look at the pictures displayed on their first pages. Why I did not read them, I don't know. I really hadn't any prejudice against them, at least from a moral point of view, nor do I think I was afraid of wasting my time over them, for I must have wasted it pretty liberally in other ways. I never heard of any boy who was whipped because he read them, but I have no doubt that it has happened."

William Lyon Phelps says:

"I certainly did read any number of dime novels in my boyhood. My favorite series was 'Jack Harkaway' — 'Jack Harkaway among the Indians' gave me all kinds of thrills. Furthermore, I used to read regularly the *Fireside Companion,* whenever it was left at the front door, as it was occasionally on a Saturday night, and of course I read scores of novels by Oliver Optic, Horatio Alger, Jr., and Harry Castlemon. I do not know of any boy who was ever whipped for reading dime novels. I did not have to read them on the sly, but I was never allowed to read them on Sunday, which was a good thing, because it made me read Bunyan's 'Pilgrim's Progress' about twenty times — that was permitted on Sunday. My father and mother frequently remonstrated with me for reading so much trash, but they did not actually forbid it during the week, although they viewed it with alarm."

Stephen Leacock writes: "You hit me where I live!" and sends this extract from his "What I Read as a Child":

"I read also — and I am only too glad to admit it — dime novels. I read a lot of them, but I cannot remember their names. I should read them still if I could get any of the kind and brand that I read thirty-five years ago. But I imagine that the plot and characters have changed. The scene of the dime novel, I remember, was laid 'on the prairie.' This was a vague conception, now hopelessly damaged by a mental picture of state boundaries and railroad maps and news items about prohibition votes in Dakota and agricultural conventions in Omaha. There may, for all I know, still be prairies, but for literary uses the prairie is dead.

"The dime novel of my early days always opened with 'Bang! Bang! Bang!' This is no longer possible with modern weapons of precision. Some one would get hit."

Frank M. O'Brien, editor of the New York *Sun,* says:
"I liked dime novels and my mother opposed my reading them. This may have been because of their supposed influence or because ten cents was considerable money in the early eighties. As for the evil influence, I cannot see that they were any worse than the *Family Story Paper* or the *New York Ledger,* both of which publications were taken into homes, read by ladies who

doted on serials of the 'Wee Wifie' brand, and left around to be secreted by me. 'Old Cap Collier piping the Stewart Grave Robbery' was a dandy. I liked the 'Deadwood Dick' series immensely and at the age of ten I had a complete list of what I would need when I went West. One repeating rifle, two six-shooters, a tomahawk and a Bowie knife. Forty years later, when I got my first opportunity to go West, the only weapon I carried was a corkscrew.

"At age twelve I struck gold. We moved to a new home, with an old woodshed in the back lot. The sons of the previous tenant had left a stack of dime novels containing 'Jack Harkaway' stories and I met that pleasant adventurer for the first time. It was six months before the cache was discovered and destroyed and by that time I had read 'em all twice. I don't believe that they affected my character any more than the 'Frank Nelson' stories. The principal difference was, I think, that Castlemon's stuff came in book form and therefore parents thought it was O. K."

E. W. Kemble illustrated "Huckleberry Finn" and cared most for pictures:

"I never read any of the yellow backs as I was not a

reading youth, but I can remember my brother, my elder by two years, sneaking the things to his room and hiding them in odd nooks and corners, and when I found one I would tear off the cover and cut the picture out. The pictures always interested me more than the text. Indians galore and trappers in fringed buckskins, most always of the Bill Cody type."

From John Cotton Dana; librarian of the Newark Free Library:

"Dime novels — which, in my boyhood, were the ones by Beadle with yellow covers, were they not? — were forbidden, but I have a distinct recollection of disobeying my orders and reading at least a few. They were passed about, more or less, among us boys. I don't recall that any boy of my acquaintance was whipped for reading them. By some chance, Ballantine's 'Wild Man of the West,' in hard covers, got into our house and all of us boys read it, and I guess all the boys of the neighborhood. If there ever was a dime novel, that was one. It was a *bound* book, so it passed as reputable!

"I wonder if I am right in thinking that boys in the smaller towns of New England at the time of my boyhood had access to many more books to read than is commonly supposed. Our own home was quite well filled with books. Not many of them, I admit, were books for boys and girls, but the Sunday-school supplied books at even as low a grade as 'Elsie.' Also, there was in town a little library, kept by a bookbinder — curiously enough. In the home of some of my companions were many desirable books which were passed from hand to hand.

"I wonder if you have an opinion as to the quality of the detective and Western stories which I now read in large quantities. Are they as far from having any literary value as were Beadle's books of old days? If they are about on the Beadle level, then I am, myself, flourishing in a second childhood with Beadle's novels, in effect."

Arthur Bartlett Maurice (under whose editorship *The Bookman* published some excellent articles on this and similar subjects) writes:

"Did I read dime novels? I'll tell the cock-eyed world I did. I think I was about eleven when I read my first. It was 'The Boy Detectives in China.' Another early one was 'Red Light Will, the River Detective.' Then came the 'Old Rafferty' series. Forbidden to read them, though with no great severity, I read them in the family circle concealed between the covers of *Golden Days,* a permitted periodical. I wish I could get a kick now out of something compared to the kick from those dime novels of the dear dead days of yore. Curiously I never read the 'Nick Carter' books. One of Oliver Optic's stands out in memory. It was 'Brian Brasslock, the Professor's Son.' I came across a copy a few years ago. The incidents were quite familiar, but of course it was dreary reading. One book, one of the very first read, left a decided impression. I cannot recall the title, but it told of a houseboat moored to the shores of Gowanus that broke loose in a storm and drifted across the bay to Communipaw. Not associating Gowanus with a part of Brooklyn, there was in the name magic, and music, and mystery. In my youthful mind it was Barbary or Far Cathay.

"But the great dime novel of my earliest years was 'The Pilgrim's Progress,' which I read, not as a religious allegory, but as a gorgeous and bloody romance. With a lathe for a sword and the top of a flour barrel for a shield I marched forth announcing that I was Greatheart about to decapitate Giant Despair."

This is from William Beebe. (The author of this book agrees with him about Kingston and Jules Verne.)

"Yes, I remember, very distinctly, dozens of dime novels, but I soon switched to those which dealt with tropical adventure. I went through all of them, being blessed with a father who did, and still does, enjoy the same things I always have. W. H. G. Kingston and Henty and G. Manville Fenn and Jules Verne stand out clearest in my mind; I have most of them still somewhere."

About one fifth of the men and women to whom I wrote, admitted, blushing and apologizing, that they never read dime novels at all.

The novels did not come their way; or they read other books, from family or public libraries (this defence is frequent from New England); or, in a very few instances, the dime novels were disapproved or actually forbidden.

Among those who never or hardly ever read the novels, are Mrs. Gertrude Atherton; Arthur Train (who read one, and forgot it); Charles Dana Gibson; M. A. DeWolfe Howe; Professor Robert Palfrey Utter, of the University of California; Joseph H. Sears, the publisher; Miss Ethel Parton and Arthur Stanwood Pier, both of *The Youth's Companion;* Gamaliel Bradford; Frank Crowninshield, editor of *Vanity Fair;* Jesse Lynch Williams; Charles Hanson Towne; Thomas Hastings, the architect; and Miss Carolyn Wells.

Let Walter Prichard Eaton speak for them. His remarks are typical of the experience of many — especially in that he might have read dime novels had he been *forbidden* to do so:

"Alas! I never read dime novels. By some process now unknown to me, my parents contrived it so that I had plenty to read (without seeking the paper backs) and exciting things, too. I rather fancy, also, as I recall it, that in the town where I lived, north of Boston, few boys had dime novels, nor do I recall that they were sold in any store in town. Anyhow, they played no part in my early youth. When I was about 13, I remember one of my friends getting hold of one and lending it to me to read. But by that time I fear I saw thro' it, and considered it poor stuff, for by then I was reading Dickens and Scott, etc. Probably I was a toploftical little snob, anyhow, for I recall holding my friend up to ridicule for reading such stuff!

"Had I ever been forbidden to read dime novels, doubtless I should have read many. But no prohibition was ever put on my reading; the library, home and public, was left open to me; and I seemed to find plenty of food therein."

VI

"BUT OUR HERO WAS NOT DEAD!"

DIME novels died in the eighteen seventies when the first series of Beadles came to an end. They died again, some years later, when postal rates caused the change from the little book to the magazine form. They died again, of too much sensationalism, in the eighteen eighties. They were killed once more by the nickel libraries and the boy's weeklies, which were themselves dime novels in a slightly changed form. They have been killed by yellow journalism, by the moving pictures, and for all I know, by the War, and by Prohibition.

Yet — go the nearest news stand, and look at the Wild Western and Detective magazines, for ten, fifteen and twenty cents. They have a strange resemblance to the dime novel.

And in foreign countries, it is said, the old dime novel is being read. In Italy, after the War, there suddenly blossomed forth:

"Nick Carter; Il Gran Poliziotto Americano."

And a series of Italian pamphlets, which I have seen, are all about "Buffalo Bill: L'Eroe del Wild West."

On the cover of one of them, in colors, is our old scout, Colonel Cody.

He has a dashing costume, of a kind likely to be useful in a tight place, on the prairie or in a canyon. He has white breeches, high, black, patent-leather boots, with enormous buckles, like those worn by Charles I. A red shirt and a handsome buckskin coat complete his outfit.

The Colonel is backed up against a precipice, looking with some concern at a lion, a puma, and a tiger, all three crouched and ready to spring upon him from a distance of not more than four feet. They are being restrained for the moment by the upraised arm of a very dignified Aztec high priest. Plainly, they will leap at his throat if the high priest gives the word.

And behind the Aztec is his steed — a supercilious camel, who regards the whole scene with the typical sneer.

THE END

APPENDIX

APPENDIX

COMMENTS ON THE ILLUSTRATIONS

"Oonomoo, The Huron." By Edward S. Ellis.

This is one of the "yellow-backed Beadles" — that is, one of the original series of dime novels, of which the first was "Malaeska," by Mrs. Stephens, appearing in June, 1860. They were published semi-monthly, and "Oonomoo" probably came out on June 1, 1862, in the height of the Civil War.

Mr. Ellis, a prolific writer of dime novels, and one of the best of them, died in 1916. He wrote, at the age of nineteen, "Seth Jones," the eighth dime novel, and the first great success in the series. It sold many hundred thousands of copies. He was also the author of many other books: histories, biographies and novels, which were published in boards and at conventional prices.

"Oonomoo" is a little, paper-covered book, about six inches high, by four inches broad, with 114 pages. In the imprint, the publishers name their London office, Number 44 Paternoster Row, from which, as early as 1862, they were issuing English editions of the dime novels, printed from the American plates.

APPENDIX

The original series of these novels, with the yellow or salmon covers, continued into the eighteen seventies, and numbered more than three hundred. The stories were from twenty-five to forty thousand words long.

The picture on the cover, "Oonomoo attacked by the Shawnees," was repeated as a frontispiece. There were no other illustrations, and a frontispiece was not invariably used. Stories of early Indian warfare in the Eastern States, and stories of the Revolution were favorites in this first series.

Number 45 of the series, "Esther," by Mrs. Ann S. W. Stephens, brought $9 at the O'Brien sale in 1920. Others of the series brought $10 or $11. "Seth Jones," by E. S. Ellis, sold for $13.

"Old Grizzly, The Bear-Tamer." By Captain "Bruin" Adams.

Beadle's Pocket Novels were the second series published by Beadle and Adams. They began about 1869 or 1870 and appeared twice a month. "Old Grizzly," copyrighted in 1874, contains an advertisement listing 240 already published, and 15 to follow.

They were nearly the same in size and number of words as the first series, but used more color on the cover. In this, the border is red and the picture is in four colors. Borders in blue, brown and green are also found.

APPENDIX

Captain Adams' name was James Fenimore Cooper Adams, and his uncle was James Capon Adams, who, although a native of New York State, was known as "Old Grizzly," from his remarkable skill in taming grizzly bears, and his *penchant* for riding about upon one.

The scenes of the novels, in this series, are moving westward, to the great plains, the Rockies, and beyond, but the pictures, although thrilling, have not reached the heights of sensationalism achieved in the next decade.

Nor has Beadle's expert in devising alliterative titles yet come into action. This series includes: "The Unseen Hand; or, The Four Scouts of the Waccamaw," by J. Stanley Henderson; "Silverspur; or, The Mountain Heroine. A Tale of the Aarapaho Country," by Edward Willett; "Nick Doyle, the Gold Hunter; a Tale of California," by Peter Hamilton Myers; and the rather curiously named sea story, "Tom Pintle, the Pilot; a Tale of the Three Years' War," by H. Milnor Klapp.

"Old Grizzly" brought $22.50 at the O'Brien sale.

"WESTWARD BOUND." By Seelin Robins.

This cover, in three colors, with an orange border, recalls the days when the American Indian, instead of being a stockholder in the railroads, actually opposed their advance, and tried to push the locomotive off the track.

The "New Dime Novels" were 6½ by 4 inches; contained thirty thousand to forty thousand words, and 92 to 100 pages. Some in the series are said to have been copyrighted as early as 1866. The highest number I have seen is Number 630, Ellis's "Phantom Horseman," copyright in 1869, but others, earlier in the series, bear copyright dates as late as 1874.

The stories are of Indian wars and Western pioneer life. Captain Whittaker's "The Death's Head Rangers," quoted earlier in this book, is an item in this series.

Dewey's "Spanish Jack," at the O'Brien sale, brought $11 and Willett's "The Gray Hunter" sold for $7.50.

"OLD RUBE, THE HUNTER; OR, THE CROW CAPTIVE." By Captain Hamilton Holmes.

"Frank Starr's Ten Cent American Novels" are publications of the house of Beadle and Adams, as Starr was their foreman, and Number 41 Platt Street was a side entrance to the Beadle factory on William Street.

This series was one of the gayest in appearance, and least like the typical dime novel. The first one of the series came out about 1870. This novel, "Old Rube," was copyrighted in 1874. One of the latest, which I have seen, is Number 216, published in 1877.

This novel is 9 inches high (some of the series were about 7½ inches high) and about 6 inches broad. It is printed in

APPENDIX

double columns, with 47 pages. The stories in this series are from thirty to fifty thousand words long. The covers are in colors; occasionally partly colored by hand, as in the red coat of the hunter in this picture.

"Captain Hamilton Holmes" is one of the pseudonyms of that prolific writer of dime and other novels, T. C. Harbaugh. He died in 1924.

Other titles in this series are: "Redpath the Avenger; or, The Fair Huntress of the Southwest," by John Hovey Robinson: "Old Tiger, the Patriot; or, The Heroine of the Mohawk," by Newton Mallory Curtis; and a number of works by the redoubtable Ned Buntline, including one with an even more than usually cumbersome title — "Saul Sabberday, the Idiot Spy; or, Luliona, the Seminole."

At the O'Brien sale, Bowen's "Scouting Dave," of this series, was sold for $10.50 and Hazeltine's "California Joe" for $25. The higher price of the latter was probably because it is semi-biographical: California Joe being a real personage.

"Roaring Ralph Rockwood, The Reckless Ranger." By Harry St. George.

Beadle's "Pocket Library" began in 1884, Number 1 being Wheeler's "Deadwood Dick." They were issued every Wednesday, at five cents apiece. The latest in date in the New York Public Library is Number 492, dated 1893.

APPENDIX

They are ragged little pamphlets, about 8½ inches high, by 6 in breadth; usually of about 32 pages; with stories from twenty-five to forty thousand words in length. The picture is in black and white. The quality of the paper is poor, and copies now in existence are usually in bad condition.

"Harry St. George" is St. George Rathborne, who was born in Kentucky in 1854. He wrote many dashing romances of love and adventure, somewhat of the Archibald Clavering Gunter school. I remember being moved to emotions of one kind or another by his "Dr. Jack" and "Dr. Jack's Wife." The price of his novels advanced, but the paper covers continued.

All the favorite Beadle authors wrote for this series, including Prentiss Ingraham, Oll Coomes, Captain Whittaker, Bracebridge Hemyng, the creator of Jack Harkaway, Philip S. Warne (about whom there was much mystery) and Jesse Cowdrick.

In this series are: "Frio Fred in Texas; or, Old Rocky to the Front," by Sam S. Hall; "Tom the Texas Tiger; or, Old Luke's Luck," by Oll Coomes; and "Picayune Pete; or Nicodemus, the Dog Detective," by Charles Morris.

Specimens of this series fetched from $2 to $5 in the O'Brien sale.

"The Scalp-Hunters." By Captain Mayne Reid.

Beadle and Adams' twenty cent novels as compared with

APPENDIX

the "Dimes," gave more than twice as much for the price. This has 208 pages, and the portrait of Captain Reid is tinted by hand. He stands against a pale-blue background, in a reddish brown coat. There are flesh tints for his face and hands; his trousers are horizon blue; there is a hint of a waistcoat in crimson lake; and his monocle is golden. The book is 6½ inches high and 4¼ inches broad.

The series began in 1871 and lasted at least until 1877, although there are only thirty-one known items in it. They had fifty thousand to sixty thousand words.

Mrs. Victor's "Turkey Dan"; Colonel Cody's "Deadly-Eye"; three or four titles by Albert W. Aiken, including "The Phantom Hand; or, The Heiress of Fifth Avenue"; and Charles Bertrand Lewis' "Mad Dan" were in this series. (Lewis was "M. Quad.")

"The Scalp Hunters" and "The White Squaw" (for the Ms. of the latter the Beadles paid their record price of $700.) were both in twenty-cent novels.

Mayne Reid was my favorite of all these writers, and his "Scalp Hunters," when I read it, some time in the early nineties, had qualities which almost totally checked the action of the heart. I still recall the parley, in the ruined mine, between the white men and the Indians.

It is rather distressing to learn that Captain Reid had a

APPENDIX

glass eye — doubtless in place of one lost on the field of honour. When he and his fellow novelists adjourned from the Beadle offices to a nearby place of refreshment, the gallant Captain had sometimes the misfortune to have his eye drop from its place, into his drink. Then, it had to be fished out before the drinking could proceed.

He was born in Ireland in 1818; he fought on the American side in our war with Mexico; he died in England in 1883; and thousands of boys have adored his books.

At the O'Brien sale Badger's "Pacific Pete" of this series sold for $11 and Aiken's "Red Arrow" for $10.50.

"DANDY ROCK, THE MAN FROM TEXAS." By G. Waldo Browne.

With Beadle's "Half Dime Library" and his "Dime Library" began the disappearance of the small books with colored covers. The new series were larger in size (the Half Dimes were 11½ inches high by 8½ broad) and looked like a cheap magazine rather than a book. They contained thirty thousand to forty thousand words. "Dandy Rock" had sixteen pages, which was the usual length, printed in triple columns of small type. They may have been the foundation of the vast fortunes owned to-day by American oculists and opticians.

At least 1067 titles appeared in this series, and if any Beadles are to-day remembered by readers, these are apt to be the ones. The striking illustrations, in black and white, are usually by George G. White, whose talents were displayed on scores of these covers, and whose ability enabled him to draw both for the *Police Gazette* and the *Christian Herald*.

They were published weekly at five cents apiece. The copyright date on Number 8 (a reprint of "Seth Jones") is 1877; and Number 1067 (Arizona Cy's "You Bet Bob's Jangle") is dated 1898.

All the famous Beadle authors wrote for this series, and the titles included Frederick Whittaker's "Dick Darling, The Pony Express Rider"; Edward L. Wheeler's "Deadwood Dick's Eagles; or, The Pards of Flood Bar"; Colonel Cody's "Fancy Frank of Colorado"; Joseph E. Badger's "Crooked Cale, The Caliban of Celestial City"; Oll Coomes' "Dashing Dick; or, Trapper Tom's Castle"; Jesse C. Cowdrick's "Disco Dan; The Daisy Dude"; and also his "Bicycle Bob's Hot Scorch" (showing the influence on dime novelists of later inventions than the mustang); Wm. G. Patten's "Violet Vane's Vow"; T. C. Harbaugh's "Branded Ben, The Night Ferret"; Jo Pierce's "Buck Bumblebee, The Harlem Hummer"; and A. K. Sims' "Kent Kirby, The High Kicker from Killbuck; or, The Roster of Rogue River Ranch."

The prices which these will fetch depend upon the individual item. Thus, at the O'Brien sale, Major Hall's "The

APPENDIX

Tarantula of Taos" brought $3.50 and Harbaugh's "Old Eclipse" sold at $4. But stories about real personages of pioneer days always commanded higher prices, probably from collectors of Western Americana. Whittaker's "California Joe's War Trail" sold for $22.50.

"CAPTAIN COOL BLADE." By Joseph E. Badger, Jr.

The name Beadle is not conspicuous on his "Dime Library." "Captain Cool Blade" is a trifle more than twelve inches high and eight inches broad. It has twenty-four pages (many had thirty-two) set in three columns, by a printer who should have been called Myopia Matt; or, The Spectacle-Makers' Sycophant. The stories in this series usually had fifty thousand to seventy-five thousand words.

The earliest which I have seen is Samuel S. Hall's "Kit Carson, Jr.," which is Number 3, copyrighted in 1878. The latest: Aiken's "Injun Dick," Number 996, dated 1897. They were published fortnightly.

There were biographical items, about Kit Carson; Wild Bill Hickok; Big Foot Wallace; and Buffalo Bill.

For the most part, the wild doings of the Wild West, trappers, ranchers, Indians, gold-seekers, cowboys, road agents and bad men were the subjects of the tales. But Colonel Ingraham, remembering that he had been soldier and sailor, too, would occasionally put to sea with "Black Beard, the

Buccaneer; or, The Curse of the Coast." Mr. Aiken would turn his eye to the northeast, from his window in Beadle's shop, and write "The Winning Oar; or, The Innkeeper's Daughter, A Story of Boston and of Cambridge, of the College Boys at Harvard, of the Great Boat Race, of Woman's Love, Man's Treachery, and Sisterly Devotion."

The Beadle expert in alliterative titles probably asked for a raise in salary after he devised Number 549; Eyster's "Belshazzar Brick, the Bailiff of Blue Blazes, or Four Horse Frank's Frolic at Bad Luck Bar."

Ingraham's "The League of Three" (with portraits of Cody, Hickok and Texas Jack) brought $11 at the O'Brien sale; Hall's "Kit Carson Jr." sold for $17. A number of other items of the series sold for $2 or less.

ACKNOWLEDGMENTS

THE chief source of information has been the Beadle Collection of Dime Novels, which was given to the New York Public Library by Doctor Frank P. O'Brien.

The catalogue of this collection, published by the library, has already been mentioned in the text of this book, and has been used constantly.

By arrangement with the publishers of this book, Doctor O'Brien has made his private collection of Beadle material — letters, pictures, books and other data — available to me, and has aided in every possible manner.

The following articles in magazines have been especially useful:

"Dime Books." By William Everett. *North American Review,* July, 1864. 99:303.

"The Dime Novel Nuisance." By William McCormick. *Lend A Hand,* April, 1890. 5:253.

"Confessions of a Dime Novelist, An Interview." By Gelett Burgess. *The Bookman* (New York), August, 1902. 15:528.

ACKNOWLEDGMENTS

"Dime Novel Makers." By George C. Jenks. *The Bookman* (New York), October, 1904. 20:108.

"The Dime Novel in American Life." By Charles M. Harvey. *Atlantic Monthly,* July, 1907. 100:37.

"A Plea for Old Cap Collier." By Irvin S. Cobb. *Saturday Evening Post,* July 3, 1920. Published in book form by George H. Doran Company. New York, 1921.

"Man Merriwell." By James M. Cain. *Saturday Evening Post,* June 11, 1927.

INDEX

INDEX

INDEX

INDEX

INDEX

INDEX